MOVING FROM
RETIRE TO INSPIRE

I'M NOW CALLED A SENIOR

WTF

JULIE SURSOK

Lifechange Productions Pty Ltd
P.O. Box 563,
St Ives
NSW 2075

I'm Now Called a Senior WTF

Cover Design by 100Covers.com
Interior Design by FormattedBooks.com

ISBN: 978-0-6487598-2-9 (Paperback)
ISBN: 978-0-6487598-3-6 (ebook)

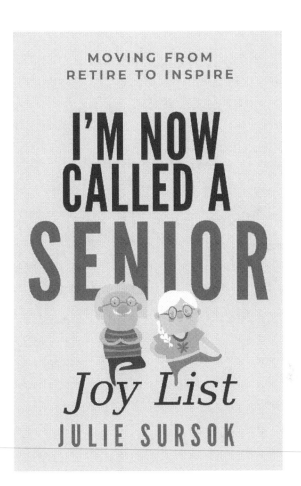

JUST TO SAY THANKS FOR BUYING MY BOOK
I WOULD LOVE TO GIVE YOU MY SENIOR'S JOY LIST

100% FREE

TO DOWNLOAD GO TO:
https://imnowcalledasenior.com/joylist

Dedication

This book is dedicated to
Co-senior,
who will do anything to make me smile…

You can't help getting older,
but you don't have to get old.

—GEORGE BURNS

CONTENTS

INTRODUCTION

Hɪ!

Let me introduce myself.

I'm Julie, and I 'get' being a senior because I am one too. Your senior moments are my senior moments — the good, the bad, and the damn right inconvenient.

However, I do not believe that passion for life needs to dissipate just because the body, brain, or society says so.

NO!

We don't need to retire from life when we retire. We are only at the starting line of myriads of new experiences, hobbies and friendships.

This book will make you laugh and cry and think and relate, and in the end, you will notice that we all have a common thread. We are not old, we are merely re-adjusting.

Of course, there will be observations that seem politically incorrect, but I know you will be quick to forgive — we are seniors, after all.

I promise to work hard at learning and evolving in the better understanding of all - always from the premise of love.

I am a passionate reader, a passionate learner, and a passionate participator in life. And with this passion, I would like to help you realize that life can still be lived very much with relevance.

Part of the proceeds of this book will go toward helping homeless seniors to find their purpose as well.

It is still very much our time!

SO.........

Get started right away Boomers. Have fun reading, and laugh out loud—VERY LOUD.

We are all in this crazy stage of life together.

We are on the same team.

HELLO BOOMERS

BOOM!

Did that wake you up, seniors?

I am one of you. So, who are we?

We are ageless.

We are strong.

We are invincible.

We are immature.

We overdo it.

We creak. (I promise only a little bit -we have meds for this.)

But here is the good news. The goal posts have now changed. It's the return of the 'silver boomerangs'.

We may sometimes think old, but *old* these days is only the commencement of 'middle age'. Not *Middle Ages*, mind you. Be careful of that one. We are much more progressive than that.

We are only one smidgeon past the beginning. We are free, uncluttered, imaginative, and absolutely where we should be.

Are you ready to BE Boomers? Really BE? Are you ready to DO? Are you ready to BECOME?

'It's too late!' you cry, as you gloomily reflect over lost opportunities.

So, what do you want, Boomers? Do you want to sit around waiting glumly for the grim, Grim Reaper to wield his scythe and wait for the last grain to fall? Or, do you want to live — yes, really live?

Our bods and brains are made to be used right up to the finish line.

I challenge you, then. Go out and be your most beautiful, bodacious, bounteous, and booming selves. Start dreaming, and action those dreams. You *can* do it all! What is stopping you?

I know, I know. Some of you are just born old. Some of you are stacking on the mileage and floating into an irrelevant oblivion of nothingness.

It doesn't have to be this way.

Let's all change and envelop ourselves in our new aging existence.

Let's allow ourselves all the 'can do' thoughts.

I know the chassis can be a bit inconvenient (and leaky and creaky), and the cerebrum floats in peanut butter now and then. I know that grey weeds march with honour over the cranium. I know the girth is defined as an 'apple', but give it right back — aren't we 'Golden Delicious'?

Forget all the nonsense out there.

Go out and play hard or soft, you significant seniors. But, for goodness' sake, throw the dice. Be in the game and play. Play with newfound, carefree freedom.

We are boomers, seniors, old-timers, Methuselahs — whatever blows our hair back (whatever remains, that is). We can't help this gradual mellowing, but come on, lovelies, let's aim at an elevated perspective. (Well, maybe not *too* elevated at this stage in our lives.)

Our days are gifted, our opportunities endless, our bucket lists full.

Let's take risks.

Let's dress inappropriately.

Let's wear red lipstick (you go, boys; you can too!).

Let's meditate deeply.

Let's laugh, cry, dance, eat, and love.

Let's hug family.

Let's choose freely.

Let's pray fervently.

It means we are relevant.

It means we are strong.

It means we are free.

It means we are alive.

'You can't help getting older, but you don't have to get old', so says George Burns.

I'm now called a Senior WTF...

BOOM!

SPRAY AND PRAY

I AM A GERMAPHOBE!

True germaphobe!

Are you a germaphobe too?

When eating out, my brain bombards me with thoughts that another mouth has sucked on the fork that I will now put into mine and I want to gag.

Galloping thoughts flood my brain.

What if the previous 'forker' has some raging virus that remains rampant on the utensil? What if I then suck on this same unclean instrument and absorb and inhale all the germs? How am I to know if the restaurant has a food-hygiene certificate because I can't see it laminated on the wall? I can only see shiny blobs of yesterday's meal reflecting off the silver and the plate in front of me is also covered in 'smooge'.

Do you see my conundrum? Does it turn your stomach too?

The worst part of this whole scenario is that my germaphobia doesn't only remain in 'restaurant land'—it's everywhere. Antiseptic wipes are my most prized go-to accessory for door handles, steering wheels, trolleys, movies, in planes, and knobs—all sorts of knobs.

Do you know how many knobs are out there and how many have been touched?

So, back to the phobia.

Co-senior was excited this morning. He had arranged to meet up with an old friend who had been absent. He was excited as he hadn't seen this friend for a while and was looking forward to catching up on all the news and developments, simply enjoying some healthy testosterone-filled company.

My day continued as planned, with no expectation of contact until the visit was over. I was certainly surprised to see co-senior's number pop up on the device.

'Babe, I promise I didn't sit too close, and I am in the gents with the "wet ones."'

That was enough to kick-start the nervous system. What the hell was going on?

'He's got "EBOLA".'

Now I was in total breakdown mode.

Ebola!?!?

This was not the Congo, Gabon, Sudan, Ivory Coast, Uganda, or Africa — this was the Antipodes, and we were not non-human primates.

I had read, though, that a case had emerged here and there. How did this friend happen to be the one case? Was that where he had been hiding the past few years? Why wasn't he locked up in pristine isolation or sharing a space with the only other known case while they were inhaling droplets together?

And now, my co-senior, my love of my life, was breathing in the roving bubbles of infection, and he was then coming home. Did this mean I had to get into full hazmat gear? And would we touch or exchange fluid ever again?

Holy moly! This was not a good ending.

Then some logical thinking evolved.

Nah, couldn't be. This ain't Ebola! He wouldn't be sitting with an ale and my husband with Ebola! Surely not!

Co-senior had recently had his hearing check, and all was A-OK. But cerumen blockage is pretty on the mark these days, confusing a few vowels. The nasty can become quite terrifying.

One would truly know if it was Ebola. 'E. coli, however, presents very differently, my darling. Still, pretty grateful that you used the wet ones.'

Poor lunch date surely must have wondered why the expanding distance at the table. Unfortunate fella must have thought his E. coli was tooting a trifle too loudly or bringing back memories of the flatmate's new cabbage recipe.

I will take ear problems any day—just don't talk about Ebola.

These lunch dates can be hilarious, actually, especially when we are all now mostly minus a decibel. Imagine the stories we recount to our partners on our return to home pastures.

Colin has bought a poodle (he is actually trying to be frugal),

Lorraine is undercover (when she has really lost her mother),

Angela is feeling pissed (actually broke her wrist), and

Doug won his club bowls competition (actually couldn't start the ignition).

There is so much going on in our friendship circle, and we can't wait to meet again to hear all the new fabulous stories.

Added into the mix we have glorious food fights.

Dentures are not holding, implants are uneven, front teeth are protruding, and sprays of masticated colour fly across the table into each other's dishes as we animatedly recount our adventures.

Diners at the next table are gagging. We are in wonderland.

Our multifocals are all over the place, and we look through the far section when we should be looking through the near. All these little sparkles of colour are now creatively dotted in our food and are missed in the blur. We happily mix and stir and joyfully shovel in the next bite.

Meals with friends these days are quite blissful, and we can't wait for the catch up again next week.

When we meet, we can laugh at the same stories, compare our ailments, and consume the same communal spit-projected blends.

Who cares if I am a germaphobe?

We do this every fortnight, our immune systems are holding up, and everything appears to be quite magnificently sterile.

Coronavirus has changed this situation but we can all still stay "virtually" connected.

TRAINS AND BOATS
AND PLANES

BEANS? WHY BEANS?

Co-senior and I are about to be encased in a mega metal torpedo (namely, a four-engine jet) for hours, and the fallout is most certainly going to be nauseatingly gaseous and unpleasant.

We will be corralled in very, very—did I say very close proximity?—and our bodily emissions will have absolutely nowhere to go.

So why beans?

Who is this gourmand menu designer with their lavish culinary repertoire, whipping up Tottori's Koura-yaki (crab meat and crab butter wrapped in egg) or Filipino Beef Kare-Kare and Bundt and—yes, you got it—beans?!

Is it only us oldies whose bowels expand midflight? Is the third scotch and soda numbing us from the outfall or maybe contributing to the bubbles? Are we oblivious of the nuclear mass of methane and hydrogen wafting through the cabin as we pop our tandem trumpets through the night?

We are so sorry, airline staff. We feel for you as you disarm the door on our arrival. We know that you are transported to foreign lands at first whiff of a waft of Cumin or Chinese Chow Mein or Boerewors tickling your olfactories.

Just shut your eyes, and visualise you were on this journey with us. You don't even need to know the flight number. The wafting odours will take you right there.

Well, that is one side of the anatomy, but what about the other?

We Boomers also have little wee problems.

We've worked hard on our pelvic floors, we have kept liquid to the minimum, we have been very fastidious with our 'just in case'. But now we just have to wee, plain and simple.

Not so plain and simple if wedged up against the fuselage.

Worse still when two aligned passengers slip off their shoes, pop their pills and snuggle in for sixteen hours, with their luminous pink 'Shhhh, I'm sleeping' masks snuffling out life.

So, now what? We just gotta go, but how do we sneak over?

I listened to my daughter and took her advice. I practice my yoga, but I can't lift my leg high enough to not touch.

I can do the wide-angle seated forward bend. I've been following my weight reduction plan consistently as I have to look perfecto on landing, but I can't fit through the microcosmic (yes, used that word as we are hurtling through the cosmos) space between the body and the headrest.

Simple.

Now I've got cramp — shit — and I'm stuck.

And what if we hit an air pocket? I will be doing a 'seated reverse cowgirl'.

Well, how does that go again?

And who designs (lots of design issues here) the small room that is used for privately accessing the sanitation fixture for urination and defecation? Mouthful isn't it!

The floor is wet — oh God, where do I stand?

I didn't put on flight socks, and there is a minute space right over there where I can pirouette between sitting and standing. Is it from the basin or a rampant penis?

And what the hell has happened to my hair (as I glance in the mirror)? It pouffed on embarkation and it has now evolved from smart and sassy to an epidemic of grey, brittle and frayed.

Oh no, the seatbelt sign is now flashing. I can't get my compression tights up.

I could slam into the ceiling or get sucked through the toilet orifice to sail into space for evermore. I'll just have to go out crutch to knee, and let's hope when adjusting it doesn't look like the 'Mile High Club'.

And final rant, I can't get my damn suitcase out of the overhead. I'm short and a bit off balance—age related, of course.

I can't stand on your seat to retrieve my errant suitcase that is cuddling with yours in the dark cavern of the storage compartment. And now, even if you are tall, as in 'defender basketball tall' or 'model who can wear anything tall', I can't ask for help for fear of a worker's compensation claim or traveller's insurance claim for a disc collapse or ripped shoulder blade from helping a little, grey old lady.

So, I will be slow. That is all there is to it, and unfortunately, your chicky babe is just going to have to wait. It takes a longggg time for this coffin dodger to regroup.

So now that co-senior and I have air travel all under control, we flitted off to Japan last month. 'Oh,' remarked everyone, 'and who was your travel agent?'

Travel agent? Moi!

Some do Sudoku, and some arrange travel. It keeps the marbles shiny and bright.

And blissful it was.

It was the interval between cherry blossoms and torrentials, and we simply were *Lost in Translation*. Eating was art, exploring was daring and Japanese customs were enchanting.

We were, however, reminded, in little tranches, that maybe we were just a little tad creakier. One restaurant in Kyoto enticed us to explore and indulge in yet another highball, while our shoes were quite happy making friends with the sneakers next door and the wobbly staircase transported us up to culinary heaven.

Surprise, but not really surprise, sitting on the floor was de rigueur. We slid down in a blink, crossing ankles with knees wide apart (sounds like a country line dance). Well, as wide apart as we could get them. We found this was not sustainable two minutes in, when toes found their spot nestled comfortably in the other one's crutch.

But what goes down has to come up, and herein lies the problem.

There are a couple of methods here.

The first is the slide-the-back-up-the-wall stance. But, paper-thin walls in heritage Japanese alleys may not sustain the good old European solidity. We found that one out pretty quickly as we slammed our backs against same walls in fits of giggles, and like two little piggies, huffed and puffed, and it almost fell down.

So, maybe then, the half-turn-on-side, push-up-with-one-hand manoeuvre. The problem is that hip bone connects to knee bone, and they don't seem to be talking to each other. Looking like an inventive Pilates-come yoga movement, it doesn't follow through. It's far too embarrassing to ask for a hand up. The charade of explanation would only end up a bit flirty.

Option three: roll over on knees, like the nightly bath ritual, bum in air. (Did we have beans? No just edamame—we are in the clear.)

All fours now. Just think greyhound ready to bolt, one knee forward.

Ahhh, just like the lunge on the wall chart, under stretches. Knuckles down, picking-up-grandchildren muscles locked, and pushhhh…

Geronimo! We are up, and we nod our heads with beaming smiles and our embarrassment hidden between a myriad of 'namastes'.

You can't do Japan without the Shinkansen. I knew that and was well prepared, confidently booking us in for departure.

Patterned letters stared at us from directional billboards. Hieroglyphics made no sense, and in good Aussie speak, we lamented loudly, 'Where the bloody hell are we?'

We learned rapidly that Japanese trains and systems are in a league of their own, a microcosm of Japan itself: on time, accurate, efficient and oooh, the excitement of making a tightly scheduled transfer.

Well, yes, but we are Boomers booming, remember, and we need perfect preparation for precision performance. That is the performance of getting on and off a very, very fast train.

Slight problem here!

Everywhere we look are neat, miniscule luggage pieces, strung over shoulders or being led by their shipshape masters. Ours are a little more wieldy. I mean, didn't I copiously boast to co-senior that I was only in one case — that, of course, including leads and maps and hair stuff and shoes and shoes and shoes?

And so said case was half the size of our usual travel accoutrement. I had done well, very well, as I clapped myself on my back in congratulation.

But still, if you are not right up front, focussed and standing on your designated 'number 8' and rushing, pulling, dragging very fast — 200 km fast — into the 'bullet', you could be in trouble. Just a reminder, Japanese train timetables are very, very accurate and will not wait for bumbling Boomers.

So, with much backward, forward, argy bargy and adhering to the rules like good little sentinels on our allocated space, we slid into the compartment. Only problem is that it was the wrong side of the compartment. They count numbers on this train backward. I don't know, maybe it's a Japanese thing.

I galloped to my seat and looked up to see *Risky Business* taking place in the gap in front of the first seat. One bright orange medium-sized suitcase and one royal blue oversized partner in crime flew backward and forward in tandem from one side of the compartment opening to the other. Following in hot pursuit was a frazzled Boomer, hanging on for dear life, while our polite Japanese co-travellers looked on in open-mouthed bewilderment. Others, while being respectfully knocked over, mouthed 'you're welcome' as they 'flat crashed' one by one into each other.

Not so on the boats.

Well, not actually boats. Huge mega-structures enveloping swarms of eager explorers. Here, elbows are well and truly greased to ward off any errant tidal wave or roaming wheelchair.

Well, where do we start with boats?

Maybe food—colourful food, varietal food, excessive food, more food, eat-as-much-as-you-want more food, stuff-it-in, go-back-again-and-again food, wake-to-sleep food, indigestion, greasy, abundant, get-your-money's-worth food. Yes, so much to gain, and that includes waistline and scales too.

And be warned, there are dire consequences to this massive festive indulgence.

The lower appendages may not cope. Blood pressure may not cope. Gall bladder may not cope. As the ruddy appearance deepens and the breathing gasps for oxygen to accommodate the visiting kilos, the realization creeps in that, unfortunately, it's pareback time, and sensible juices, skim milk and vegies become part of the dietary repertoire. Not forgetting the circuit training on the top deck, of course, in full view of the helipad for, just in case, if the heart says, 'That's it—it's enough.'

Cruises are dwelling places in paradise—most of the time.

Between the self-satisfaction of higher-tier membership and complimentary 'top ups' of cognac, we relish in personal name terms with lounge hosts who pimp and preen for an enlarged pro-digious gratuity.

Boomers rule on ships, I say. Or think they do.

This illusion, however, is smashed when returning, a bit slip and slide to the cabin, followed by a string of stringy adolescents who take pride in surreptitious verbal abuse while charading the Boomers' shuffle to each other. They loudly note the cabin door, ready for knock-on-the-door nighttime games of hourly 'call and drop' interruptions during the night.

We Boomers never fear. Remember, in most cases, we do hold the purse strings, and if you don't play by the rules—a little off centre, we will accept sometimes—you will be eating steamed broccoli in your cabins, and the fun space will be securely cordoned off where we will be downing vodka cappuccinos and bopping and hip hopping to Abba.

Don't you just love those tippy tappy feet—the tippy tappy Boomers that have invested their pensions in the ballroom-danc-ing mania? At the first tinkle or beat, they leap to their feet. Sticks are thrust aside, strappies are already buckled and up they go to show their divine precision. I mean, where else can one practice the moves?

Oh, and heaven forbid Mr Senior forgets the step, and Madame Senior shows her despotic inner self and shoves and kicks until the formation has regrouped. And the rest of us watch in delight, sip-ping our Salty Chihuahuas.

The elevators are yet another adventure. One could read *Shan-taram* in its entirety while waiting, and when a negligible eentsy space presents itself in elevator number 16, one needs to walk in with purpose and hold in the remnants of the '100-variety buffet' belly so the elevator door can close. Heaven forbid that someone vaporizes before the doors open—and that could easily happen.

We are all seniors, after all.

NURSE AND PURSE

I HAD LUNCH WITH ONE OF MY SCHOOL FRIENDS THE other day.

Now, if we are talking school friends, that is a friend who goes way, way back and we know plenty 'mucho' about each other.

This friend has had a rough time. Her husband died suddenly in bed next to her just as they were on the precipice of diving into new adventures and travels and bucket lists.

It was heart-wrenching seeing her try to work through this, for her to find a new normal now, not as a long-attached couple but as newly single.

I have been very lucky with my co-senior. I was dumped unexpectedly in a marriage, which seems like a lifetime ago. I then married my sweetheart, becoming a threat to many who so wished that they had exactly what we had found.

So, my experience of the new dating world was pretty virginal, but as close friends, it was an easy question to ask. My friend tells me it is tough out there.

I promised I would never use the term 'when we', but maybe in this instance, I can be forgiven.

There is definitely a phenomenon of dating 'then' and now. All the social rules of dating have changed and, for us Boomers, can be a touch confusing.

Our social soirees were the meeting place where flirtatious verbal intercourse enticed a partner and prospects of further liaisons. It would then move on to acute interrogation by a parental figure or family member as to the suitability of a further alliance and, once committed, took an almighty effort of tact and grace to disentangle without hearts being broken.

Times have changed. Couples marry later, if at all. Social expectations are nil. A 'blind date' could mean that one of the partners is physically challenged, and meeting in a bar, even if it's a walk by to see if the Tinder date matches the profile, is pretty much par for the course.

Internet dating is the way, with far too many profile pics from way back then. With so much competition, who wouldn't put their best pic forward?

It's all about the 'feels' and one-night bonks without further commitment, and it seems to be just fine.

How on earth, then, do we Boomers now fare on these dating sites? We are so ill equipped for this form of dating.

So, going back to lunch with my friend.

Now that she has settled into singledom and still feels young (as in sixty, young- isn't this the new middle age?), she feels it is time to get herself out there again, to find her 'rosella' who will walk, gym, travel, love, and share a tot in the evening with her.

She tells me she has tried the internet dating avenue. It doesn't seem to be successful. There are a multitude of beautiful gals out there, so Monsieur has a plethora of choices. He is not, however, really looking that hard, as his best friend has now 'karked' it, and his best friend's wife is now his best friend and rolls up frequently at the front door with a hot lasagne and plumped and painted lips.

Then there are the various contacts made over coffee. But the thought of jumping into the sack with any of them brings on an arthritic convulsion and a quick excuse to rush home for a dose of Voltaren and Valium.

I suggested, in my innocence, that a community is important in moving on and meeting people in likewise situations. I suggested she could find a strong social network and new friends who would be supportive and fun to be around.

Golf was one suggestion, which she has taken up enthusiastically and joined a snooty up-market establishment with fees that would surpass a yearly mortgage. From some research, it appeared that it would be a case of getting fit to run very fast in the opposite direction, as partners were thrilled to imbibe with lonely singles, relieved to be away from their day-to-day partners who stayed at home and hated golf.

Well, I do sympathize with those stay-at-homes, actually, as the result of the nineteenth hole can be pretty brutal and bring home much more than whatever departed that morning, in the form of mushed-up, half-digested food mixed with stomach juices.

Then, I suggested church as an avenue for respectful, good values. 'Oh, my goodness', she said, 'I could go to church for the pickup, but how do I tell him after the second date that I don't believe in God?' Well, that was a dud.

I tried bridge, walking, sewing, courses, gardening, and more, but wasn't winning really in any scenario.

It seems that herein lies the problem.

It appears that Mr. Boomer has a truckload of physical ailments when over the middle line and is probably rattling and drowning in the numerous intake of prescription drugs for cholesterol, blood pressure, arthritis, vitamins of course and don't forget to mention Viagra.

He is also on a determined quest for Queen Boomeress to rescue him, if only to remember in which compartment to put the daily medication and drive him to his monthly appointment to the podiatrist to conquer the growth of toenails that have merged with the shoe.

The darlings are single, divorced, or widowed.

The singles—perpetual bachelors, I would say—would probably need to be avoided unless there is a crazy love spark. They have never found their nirvana to sit and watch a sunset with, and they would most probably love to navigate their life just the way it is. Change would be a very uncomfortable advancement.

The divorced are a mess.

They are angry or back in the '60s with their wild sexual flings. Well, maybe not so wild these days. It sounds romantically evolved but is not steeped in realism, as they need a little help in the underground department.

They also really need to learn how to schedule their lives.

It's our generation, remember, and they are probably sorely in need of some instruction on generalities like cooking, washing, and cleaning, and most likely the younger the better would attract, as they would have these add-on capabilities.

They also have to share their worldly goods, as they promised in marriage, and are slightly more reserved in splashing out on luxuries—or even now have none to splash out. They find new dalliances very comfortable if they find that special one who has a bit of wealth stashed away for rainy days.

All us Boomers have worked hard, indulged and loved our families to excess and, probably to their detriment, as they try to find their own way without us as their safe harbour.

We don't really need a partner to validate our wonderful selves or have someone else define our identity.

We don't need to be a nurse.

We don't need to cough up the gold bullion.

We don't need to wash undies and dirty socks.

We don't have to think about what to cook or eat or have morning coffees with someone.

But then again, my friend says that we sort of do.

Life is lonely after change, and if only, if only, if only there was someone special to share those morning coffees with, life would be wonderful.

I look at my co-senior, and I say, 'I am so grateful' and 'thank you'.

P.S. Written from a heterosexual perspective but is meant for all relationships — whatever blows your hair back.

FAILURE
TO LAUNCH

SOME OF US HAVE KIDS. SOME OF US DON'T.

Those who dreamed about having kids and were rewarded spent younger years euphorically treasuring their little 'mini mes'. We donated our best years to share in the dreams, hurts, successes, and failures. We indulged in each season of growth and arrived at seniorhood—and voilà—we survived.

For you, 'our treasures', the grand age of independence arrived. That big eighteen. The empty vodka bottles filled up with water in subterfuge, and the frantic 100-metre sprint in dangling undies to dump the garbage for clubbing money was now well and truly over.

Independence shone its vivid light, and the world beckoned for launch. Of course, free board and lodging was par for the course, which did, of course, include mountains of sports gear piled into the family wash and favourite nourishment in abundance.

Didn't it make Pappa and Gagga happy to see you so healthy and well looked after? Well, of course it did, my darlings. We may have crossed the line to the other side of ageism, but we were also young once, you know.

I couldn't wait to pound the pavement of independence when I was your age.

How liberating to sleep when I wanted to and dress, do, learn, create, and 'friendify' whenever I pleased.

I packed my bags more times than you would ever know.

The vision of singular independence enticed extraordinarily, and it was only when an offer of help to pack those same bags to launch came that the realisation of survival kicked in. And, I hadn't even then sensed the glee that was behind the assistance as my parents contemplated their own senior independence.

So why do we have children when we want them out at an 'outable' age? Aren't families meant to share life together in one homogeneous bubble?

In some cultures, it is seamless to lodge multigenerationally.

In others, manipulative discussions begin for an offer of a quick draw on superannuation funds of senior financier, allowing for the financing of a first home or an after-the-split-up-where-do-I-go-to-now home.

And finally, there are the 'sit tighters' — they will never attach their launch boosters. They are sitting tight at 'casa de los padres'. They are happy to be the bottom slice in the sandwich.

Doesn't the bottom slice get all the sauce?

Part of our souls are itching to launch these little fruits of love. We want our little offsprings to sprout their wings so we can find ourselves again. We want to be crazy. We want to experience experiences again. We want a hot bath and rumble in every room in the house — and as an aside, we don't want to listen to your rumbles as well. The nest is now a little clustered, and we want to nudge you out gently. Not because we don't love you, of course, but that little tingle of luminary independence is pricking, and we are taking notice.

We are, however, a little confused, so forgive us. We don't feel that comfortable about you exploring the Third World with no contact or protection. Nor do we want to hear our brains swoosh as the silence cripples our heart strings. We want you there — never to leave. We want the loud, noisy, everything about it, but we also want the tidy, independent singular sense of control.

It's a learning experience for us all, so let's take some gradual steps. Don't make it too sudden, as we have to re-establish our boundaries, and it takes just a little bit of time to learn, once again, how to explore our hopes and dreams for our future. We don't want to be lonely, and we don't want to be sad.

We've had to take out a room in a storage unit, as you still have so much of your stuff at home. Do you really need your Year 3 poster or your mouldy talent school tutu? Ah, but those old pics bring back so many precious memories, and that's why we neatly repack into cardboard and return to their home on the top shelf.

Hardship does sometimes smack from nowhere, and home is the only remedy. That is, first home — birth home. It's the life breath just for a while for Pappa and Gagga to recall traditions and annuls of family history. But our senior marbles are not yet clouded, and we will gently give you time to breathe, boost your confidence, and set you up for a relaunch.

Don't you want that, or is the world so buffeting that first home is the only safe place of solace and deep breath?

We are, however, now all adults in the home.

As adults, we all have opinions, likes and dislikes, different time clocks, and friend influences, and the mantle of authority vacillates between old and young bulls as they wrestle for supremacy. It shouldn't really be like that, but we are all still animals, right? We tread carefully between the line of friend and foe — the line so thin and precarious that a single step either way could tip the balance.

We promise to avoid guilt trips as you forge your own friendships and don't want to barbeque with our friends.

A knock at the front door is always a joy; home is always your home.

We are there when you boomerang between episodes in your life—it's not a white flag of defeat.

You may even find that we won't revert to our 'bringing up kids' home rules', and you will get to really know us as friends and contemporaries rather than authoritarian rule setters.

We can teach the family about our history and traditions, but don't be surprised when you do arrive home to find that your room is now the 'nude room' with all its gadgets.

You could even boomerang home to your own home—your adult independent home—coz that is where you belong.

P.S. We don't feel guilty, and we still love and adore you.

VIRTUAL BABYSITTING

—

IT'S 6:30 P.M. ON THE DOT. IT'S COUNTDOWN TIME...

3, 2, 1... 'Hi, Gaaaaaagaaaaa!'

'Helloooooo my booba lubber shnucker beautiful two-year-old grandson. It's your Gagga, lugger, shnucker boobooo lubba here.'

'Where are you?'

'I'm here, Gagga...'

'What's my yum-yum angel boy eating tonight? Ooh, nummy nummy! Mummy made you yummy yummy.'

Yip, it's virtual babysitting time, and it's right on schedule.

It's sit in front of iPad, eating dinner, 'chatting to Gagga' time.

OK, I am sort of thrilled.

It is so worth it all for that wide beam of recognition, but I may only have a few seconds before it's 'Pappaaaaa! Where's Pappppppaaaaa!?'

Now, listen here, my boy. I'm your Gagga. I'm the one who rocks you to sleep and jiggles and sways you to African lullabies. I'm the one who is on poo duty and drowns you in pacifiers when the going gets tough. I'm the one who sings Wiggles, plays Elmo, and kisses those chubby cheeks all over—so what's this 'Pappa?'

I know Pappa's wobbly cheeks are your external stimuli, and his 'where's Pappa gone?' keeps you glued, and Mrs. Doubtfire seals the deal.

'No, bubba, he isn't in the iPad. Don't you remember, bubba, Gagga plays Mr. Boink Boink and tells you stories about how Mr. Chomp eats up all the fishies?'

Oh, maybe I shouldn't repeat that one coz you did look very concerned. But I'm your Gagga, and I do have some skin in the game.

'So where's Mumma? I think I can hear her in the background—I think that was a trickle. Has Mumma snuck off to have a shower?'

'OK, bubba, be careful now. Not quite sure where Mumma is…'

'What is that in your hand? Is that a banana—is that piece of banana round? Push that to the side, bubba.'

YouTube (directed at grandparents in the 'save the baby' segment when choking) told us anything round was not good.

'Little bites, now, little bites.'

'No spit it out—thuuu, thuuu. That's right, you don't like "nahnas."'

'Good boy. Gagga is here.'

'Baby Shark, doo doo doo doo doo… '

Where the hell is Mumma?

'And now your "cuzzie" is on the line and she wants to speak to Gagga, so we will have to end, my boy.'

'Gagga loves you.'

'Hello, my poo poo.'

'What? OK, I won't call you poo poo. How about *treasure?*'

'Mmm, mmm, yes, I will have a bite. Gagga is here. Gagga's mouth is open.'

'Oh, OK, now I can't see you, treasure—wipe the "ikey" off the screen. That's a good girl.'

'No, I won't tell if you get another one—lars lars one—you promise.'

'Where's Mummy?'

'Well, yes, I love your pink unicorn helmet, and yes, Gagga will get one too when she comes over to visit. We will be same-same, my angel.'

'No, don't let Sydney lick your "ikey" — it's now yucky.'

'So, who is your best friend at school, my treasure?'

'Oh, Daniel! That's a nice name. Ohhhh, he's your 'bessss fren' Oh, there he is. Hello, Danny —'

'Oh, OK, treasure, it's Daniel, not Danny.'

'Sweetheart, I don't think it's a good idea for you all to take your clothes off. I know your "ikey" dropped everywhere, but that's OK.'

'Are those Daddy's *Star Wars* lightsabers?'

'No, I wouldn't do that darling. That luminescent blade of magnetically contained plasma can cut, burn, and melt through most substances.'

'Oh, you don't understand. OK, are you Chewbaccer or Yoda?' — *Oh, you do understand that. Daddy has been teaching you well.*

'Well, just be careful, treasure — that's Mumma's favourite picture frame. You see, treasure, there is a picture there of all of us, just our little tribe, and nothing should ever break that.'

'What was that crack? Oh, you just smashed Danny's — I mean Daniel's — blade.'

'OK, well maybe that's enough. Come and talk to Gagga.'

Where the hell is Mummy?

'What does my treasure really, really want for her birthday?'

'Barbie, Rainbow Barbie, snuggly cuddly fluffy doggy? — you know your mamma had one of those until all she had left was an ear?'

'No, don't like? OK, you want a Naboo N1 Starfighter? What the hell is that?'

'Oops — treasure shouldn't swear.'

'Well, Gagga will go and look for that and, treasure, no, no, no—you can't put Daniel's foot in the toilet. It will go 'round the bend', and we will all go 'round the bend.'

'Oh, you've found the *end* button.'

Hope you are still alive.

MEDICAL CHECKS

Our little terrier was terrified of the vet.

The mention of a car trip was his 'stress bomb'. It was as though he could smell the ether from the warmth of his basket and 'blanky' at home.

The result of this anguish was the dog 'vom' mop up in the car, even after numerous platitudes to calm his shivers.

We always travelled well-armed for this expected eventuality, and we ourselves were also on standby should a human reaction to a doctor's visit produce the same result.

I get how he felt. Shiny white-coat syndrome is a thing, especially for the daughter of a surgeon father.

Latrophobia is not pretty. We are intelligent, experienced Boomers, are we not? Tests are part of continued good health, are they not? We know that, but did we do all this checking thirty years ago?

Maybe we just have more time now to think and loop on the spaghetti tube hookup and send up the silent prayer that the metronome heartbeat monitor stays constant. Beep… beep… beep.

My Google searches say I am always in trouble. My imagination is always running wild, and I am quite convinced that I will never survive to my fiftieth anniversary.

So, question to myself: Aren't we only meant to visit doctors when we are sick? I'm not sick, so why am I torturing myself?

My blood pressure is up, and I know I need to remedy this. I didn't have my morning coffee, as coffee raises blood pressure (Google told me that).

The combative neighbour is enough to elicit an emergency visit. But, dear doctor, this is only temporary, so don't write that script for medication.

Is my cholesterol up? Did the gorging on the feast of cholesterol-laden crab contribute? Maybe if I drink a bottle of water—laced with lemon, of course—before the appointment, everything will 'go alkaline' and go down.

And note to myself, when the python tightens around my upper arm, it's time to deeeeeep breathe and think of nothing—or maybe just a tiny bit of still water and long baths and the Cook Islands. Well, maybe not the Cook Islands—I'd have to fly to get there, and I am scared of flying! Damn, now I have stuffed up the blood pressure test.

Why can I hear my heartbeat through my wrist? And QUIET... SHHHHH... SHUT UP... STOP TALKING—I think it missed a beat.

These annual health checks! Do we have to?

Do we really have to go through this whole gamut EVERY SINGLE YEAR?

The list never ends—boobs, pelvis, eyes, ears, teeth, feet, colon, pap, blood pressure, cholesterol, onions, tomatoes, eggs... oops, sorry, my two lists got mixed up again.

I suppose it's just got to be done. The kids need us as babysitters. We have countless adventures to enjoy and we don't want to exist at half-mast. We want the whole bloody body to be present.

So, the plan is to do it all in one week then 'Chivas' out at the end of it.

We need distraction paraphernalia. Zen music, yoga mat, self-help book, Philip Stein watch, knitting and, of course, rescue remedy, and if nothing else works, a little Valium popped into the purse for emergencies. This is just pre-prep, darlings. The best is still to come.

These tests are important, so pick up the phone and dial...

Well, yes, this does become a sticking point. The reminder notice embedded in the phone's alarm is interrupting the solitude on a regular basis. The sticky note in the diary is obliterating important dates. There are reminders everywhere so just...

PICK UP THE PHONE AND DIAL...

And then, just when the courageous lion emerges, reigning in the fear, it is exactly the right time to remember that there are many events coming up that just cannot be cancelled.

You don't want your life to be cancelled, you scaredy-cat Boomers. You don't want your eye pressure to win you the major role in the next Steven King movie, do you, Boomers?

JUST PICK UP THE PHONE AND DIAL...

I know all these medical checks are not fun. Who likes to sit in the waiting room with several other nervous nannas 'ducklegging' under their chairs while vacantly reading the latest newspaper with a large 'Do Not Remove' sticker all over it?

We're not actually reading it (if you are watching us); we are observing the last patient at the counter with her large envelope of X-rays waiting for the doctor's apologetic explanation of the grey shadows, and we shiver in sympathy.

The radiographer gives instructions.

I'm not listening, Wonder-Woman. I can't stop looking at the new contraption that will circle my puppies. Does it squish or just squeeze, and why are the last patient's films still stapled to your wall?

Is that black splat on the right-hand side anything sinister, or are those my last radiation pics that you are intimately comparing?

I know I am babbling on incoherently.

It is only nerves.

I've told you all about my new book, *No Sugar*.

I've told you all about my husband's new business.

I know you don't care if my nipple has shrunk or is inverted or points to the left.

For you, it's just another day.

For me, I have to wait for the machine to squash my boobs—while pretending to be oh so causal—to pancake status and in doing so rip the muscles from under my arm.

Then I have to smile patiently as you traipse off down the passage to find a bigger film and a thyroid guard I have requested.

Do I still have to hold my breath?

Maybe that is why there is a shadow on the film—I just took a breath.

Don't catch my hair on the support plate or rip it out. I don't have all that much left now, so each hair has its own story of life and death.

And then, I endure the torment of that tiny little waiting room as you are in consult. My 'tatas' are peeping out of the blue gown reading the same home decorator magazine that is left in the room, once again with 'DO NOT REMOVE'.

I am an expert on the latest yellow cushions and brown carpet trends that have been dog-eared by every previous participant. Maybe this decorating trend has boomed, as we are all reading that same article in that same waiting room in our nervous anticipation.

Why are you taking so long?

That is it. I know it. You have found something (inner scream). You have summoned all the other experts for collusion of diagnosis.

Maybe I shouldn't have drunk soymilk for so long. Maybe your guys are talking to my guys to discuss a plan. Maybe…

And it doesn't stop there—it moves onto the ultrasound. I am working hard at manipulating this angel just to give me a tiny, tiny hint that I will be sailing toward the Maldives horizon next week with all body parts beautifully intact.

Pap smear!!!

Well, Boomers. We *are* older. Do we still have to prep the night before? Shave legs, shave vag! Do we need to worry about the grey? Do we need to book a Brazilian?

I used to think this was a hunky, tanned young Adonis or, yes, I know, the latest hair straightener. But I was quickly educated in the removal of the hair phase of the day.

So, who does this now?

The skin is thinner, everything rips, everything itches and perfume stings.

Come on now, we are all girls. We have the same bits, so why do we feel even the slightest embarrassment? (Sorry, boys, if you are reading this.)

Now we have to take it all off. Damn, I should have had that tummy tuck.

The docs are pretty cool when they reassure that 'even the Queen does this'. On reflection, yes, she would have—and just a sideline, 'even the Queen poops'.

We are all in this together. Thank you, Ben Lee.

Teeth!!!! Feet and teeth, so they say. They are yielding to years of mastication. Yes, I said 'mastication', and now they are buckling from overuse. Could we claim it as a fashion statement?

The enamel is starting to creep up. Hello, Dentine, where have you been hiding for sixty-five years?

And now we have to research the numerous products offering regrowth and white enamels while they hide their ugly little ingredients that could be used to wash the floor or in printing ink.

The 'uppers' smile is important to hide the mangled mess down below. It isn't good in a selfie — more like a Halloween accessory.

And eyes…

THOUGHT I WOULD HELP YOU OUT RIGHT NOW.

Yes, it's a pair of specs for longsighted and one for nearsighted. And then something in between if we are brave enough to tackle multifocals.

The neck is put to good use trying to find the sweet spot and submission into blur when it all gets to be too much.

There are drops for this and drops for that and machines for this and machines for that. And dilation and dizziness and light sensitivity and dry eyes and patches and injections and laser.

It's the eyes' fault for being so close to the brain.

And then we lose our glasses. We are meant to put them in the same place, but we can't remember where that same place is.

Are they down the side of the car, under the sofa, on the bathroom ledge? And OOPS — whose glasses are these? I would say someone who also is going through the same hide-and-seek experience.

By now, my neck has seized up in its search for ergonomic eye level.

Bring on the laser with the terror of vapor-fine density, blurring the vision permanently. I would say the flock of blackbirds that have recently come to visit is OK right at this moment.

The skin is the largest organ of the body. So, there is a lottttt to check here. Stories spew out at every dinner party — stories of lumps and bumps and squiffy edges and kaleidoscopic patches. Question — there is skin everywhere, so how does the skin doc check *everywhere*?

Can they get to between the butt cheeks and under innovative hair streaks and in nostrils and close to the vagay? Do worrisome little patches even sprout in this natural underground chamber that's been safe for sixty-five years? Who lies in the sun for ten minutes each day, pulling the elastic aside for this little safe hideaway to get its daily dose of vitamin D?

And feet. What is the lump on the side of the foot? Where does that extra growth come from? I know it's admonishment for the '70s five-inchers or the vanity evening shoe squeeze.

And why are the toenails heaven facing? Is it a spontaneous upward curl, a compass facing north in preparation for moving up into the spatial universe?

Well, it's not every toenail; some grow inward. These ones are hardy. They remind me I'm still alive, but these are the ones that need specialist attention. These are the ones that help me find my community in the podiatrist's waiting room. These are *The Nail Brigade*.

And now I can't walk up the f*!cking stairs. These stairs used to be the stairway to heaven. We used to follow the tulip trail up the stairs de-robing an article per step, and now we can't f*!cking walk up them!

Our *abductors* used to have another meaning. Yes, please abduct me and ravish me and engulf me and now, the Abductor — it's in the same region, but it's overstretched or something, and I now CAN'T WALK UP THE STAIRS.

It's time to lock into the memory bank that when we downsize, it is never, never with stairs.

It needs to be one level, but nothing else can be one level.

We are still up for it, seniors.

SENIORS RULE.

DOWNSIZING

Channel 7 this morning was spruiking Nirvana.

Move north to Queensland they said. Buy a home for half the price of the 'bling bling' down south. Make friends, find community, eat, drink and be merry. This is, of course, aimed at us — us Boomer downsizers who are tentatively holding onto our family memories while destroying our knees in the upstairs, downstairs rollercoaster.

Sounds pretty amazing, really, until having a long think about it in my journeys around town today. I asked myself, *What would be a deal breaker?* It all seemed to form a long straight path to…wait for it… isolation and loneliness.

You see, Nirvana it may seem, but would the view and the 'old' new compensate for the old, old friends with history and countless recounts of 'when we'? It would be like your soul is emigrating again. No, that's a deal breaker for me.

I need that smell of familiarity that brings comfort. I need that vibrational frequency of all of us being on the same wavelength. I need the laugh that just gets it. I need the comfort of years of piecing the puzzle together, forming the palette of our life's history that can be shared at any time.

So, what next?

We are all in it—should we, shouldn't we, when should we, market's up, market's down. It's all too hard; wait another year.

Everyone has their own path.

My physio says, 'DO IT.'

His patients haven't moved because madame couldn't live without tending her garden planting the flowers of tomorrow from the seeds of yesterday. And now her arthritic fingers work only with lathers of ibuprofen, and she can't see the wood for the trees (ha ha, thought you would like that one).

Unfortunately, the body shrinks into oblivion, and watering the garden is the last important thought. Now it's more about making it to the bathroom in time before everything has been watered.

So, the process starts.

What is all this stuff we have?

Now that we have brilliant clarity and cleareyed vision, why the hell do we have so much stuff?

Desperate calls to kids as potential dumpees doesn't work. Nooooo, we don't want your china salt and pepper dogs that you bought in Hong Kong. It's your memory, not ours. We would rather have the old frames of your glasses as you wore them at our final concert. That's what they say.

So eBay, Gumtree, council pickups, Ziilch, friends? Where to start? And which room? And NO, I can't get rid of that.

Why on earth not?

You wore it thirty-five years ago; it has shoulder pads, for goodness' sake, and it wouldn't even fit Barbie.

Funny how when it goes, one never pines.

Sort of works the same way with moving houses.

When did you last go back to the house you lived in before the previous previous previous house? In fact, co-senior and I did have a little detour this week — just for fun — and to get away from the fumes of the backburn in our area.

Driving past the house, I wasn't remembering the lovely kitchen and bathrooms. I was thinking about when we made out on the balcony with a cheroot hanging from our lips, modelling James Dean and Marlene Dietrich.

Well, back to previous previous house memories.

Never ever have I had a nightmare 'jerk' about a long lost house. So why the reticence in moving from this one now?

I think I get why.

It's not about the house; it's about the memories formed in the house. It's about the emotions spent and the valleys and mountains in this house. It's about bringing up a family and their friends in this house. It's about *Risky Business* strips and gyrations with the mop as *Mrs Doubtfire*. It's all that and more.

That's why it is hard. And we all have these wrenches to bear!

But then, where to?

We thought it would be city side. We had spent our lives in business bedlam, with crowds and commerce and 'fairy lights'. (Our business was right in the middle of the carnival lights.)

The solitude of home after these manic periods was serenity and tranquility in the bowels of suburbia. But now that we are seniors, this suburban sluggishness can become malaise, and our brains and bodies can slowly morph into remote triviality.

But our vision of ferries to see *Rigoletto* and *The Book of Mormon* are smashed when reading about unfiltered smokestacks that will spurt harmful debris and contaminants into our body engines if we live too close to the city. Not even the beautiful views and sunsets will justify our constricted airways.

So there is always the offshore option.

Either live off the smell of an oil rag or join the swelling expat community who have succumbed to the allure of the paddie fields of Ubud or *visado de residencia* of Spain. One can always come back if it doesn't work out. Question is, penny pinch at home or live the life of indulgence as we move through age-related denial? In this bold migration, will the dream match the reality? Yet another iron to put in the fire and cause for further considerable confusion.

So then, we concur with all our fellow seniors.

We all want to leave our present and move closer to relevance. But we are accustomed to our spatial abodes where we can elbow our co-seniors into second bedrooms when the freight train of slumber takes over. We are used to the second wardrobe to house our seasonal spoils and the choice of colours to decorate our dining tables when guests arrive.

So, will a 2-1-1 fit the bill? Will we really adjust to laptop on the lap and GoGet or GreenShare or Uber?

I know, this does sound very entitled, but *one car*?!

No way, Jose. That's my independence gone, decamped, and just for the aside — my last order from UberEats was munched by someone almost in another state as GPS directions became too hard.

So back to the abode. Needs to be 3-2-2, but these are snapped up like an arrow from a bow.

Bullseye — 2.8 mil.

Seriously, that would buy a whole village if we just moved north. And then apartment blocks, strata fees, elevators, cabbage aromas. Nah, not unless on one level. I mean, the whole level, and then possibly it may work. Oh, my goodness, this sounds even more entitled!

My dream has always been high windows, water views, streamlined kitchen and equipment. A call-the-oven-from-the-golf-course-and-have-your-meal-ready-at-home sort of place. In your dreams. But we can all dream, can't we?

But what the hell would that take out of the home sale? It would mean heavy re-mortgaging, and that won't happen, as the bank won't give us a mortgage since we are not receiving a *regular monthly income*.

But, protesting wildly, we are entrepreneurs—nothing is regular. It is either pretty damn fantabulous or fudgenubbits, badgummit bad.

Of course, there is the over-fifty-fives' haven—meals sorted, health care sorted, bus trips to shopping centres sorted.

It's all about the lifestyle (or death style) companionship, bowls tournaments and—eureka!—even aqua aerobics at nine every single morning to keep the spinal spaces fluid and limbs still capable of walking.

But, hey, over fifty-five and an hour of aqua aerobics don't work perfectly in tandem, as a few spurting perpetrators slip out between the high kicks and splashes.

The ads show gleaming, white-haired Rotary companions who look oh so content as they stretch in tai chi classes and paint together—jolly jolly—and, of course, line dance on Saturday nights.

I love this for some, but I still want to kick goals from way past the midline, and I can't be a try scorer from this angle just yet.

Just as an aside, though, these over-fifty-fives are becoming more 'resorty' and less final 'destinationy'.

So, it may be a glimpse into a favourable future—just one tiny eeny bitsy step at a time.

EXERCISE — PLEASE DON'T HURT ME

—

MY DAUGHTER TELLS ME THERE ARE CENTENARIANS WHO look half their age at her gym, in her yoga class, running around parks, and hiking up canyons. They lift their legs ballerina style above their heads and balance on their scalps with not a minute of stiff.

Whoop! Whoop!

These gals are not cuddled beneath toasty blankets, wiggling their appendages for exercise, but still seriously impress with their manoeuvrability and divineness.

I was only watching Carol Burnett at the Golden Globes, eighty-five and still in the game. And then, Christie Brinkley, who my daughter gently reminds me is my age — I mean where do her long legs stop, and when will she stop looking like the *Sports Illustrated* cover model?

So, let's be real.

First reaction is it's not fair, the genetic distribution is uneven, and she got the bulk of non-aging genes. Second reaction is to jump onto Instagram profile and see how she does it and then groan to see that 'spinning classes' are her thing. Spinning classes?

The tiny seat would disappear into my intergluteal cleft, and it would probably take a rapid visit to emergency care to extricate.

So, if I want to live till I drop, it's time to take action.

Off to Zumba…

The first dilemma is what to wear. Does a long tee over track suits pants suffice, or is it the whole psychedelic look in luminous activewear? Do I need to take a trip to lululemon and Lorna Jane to kit out?

The tush looks like the sausage dog head that the magician created at the grand chillies last birthday party. It definitely needs cover at this early stage of discovery. Then midriff top—hmm, what do they mean *XL?*—it doesn't fit over the bobbles, and compression is so forceful. It reminds me that I better book lymphatic drainage this week, as there is potent lymph backup starting to happen.

Nah, orange peel needs to remain in the kitchen—don't think it is for public exposure.

So back to Zumba…

It's sort of OK to stand at the back, stepping rather than jumping, with little 'whatever' shrugs to left and right to grab my rightful place amongst sweat and 'Oh yeah'.

Co-senior waits outside to see if he needs to pick up the pieces.

'No problem', I chant as I stride out of the class and jump into the car.

Big problem as I gingerly extricate from vehicle.

What happened in the twenty-minute ride home?

Did the muscles have a starching? Why the hell are the soles cleaving to the pavement as they shuffle to the front door?

Maybe a little slower next time.

So how about ballroom dancing? That surely will have benefits, especially as co-senior reluctantly agrees to participate despite a gammy knee and there is, of course, a great Thai restaurant downstairs open on dancing days.

Ballroom dancing—so much fun if you wear the right shoes. It's difficult to salsa in runners, but runners are the only shoes that absorb the orthotics effectively with zero risk of plantar fascia complications. But salsa turns for us create a completely new salsa movement that needs to be quickly registered as intellectual property.

Experts in the field fly to the other side of the room in a haze of spin, resplendent in their dancing heels and ready for their show-offs on the dance floor of their next cruise.

So, it's time to dig out the old well-heeled beige dancers we wore thirty years ago. They have unfortunately been hiding away for a very long time. But—hooray!—the feet haven't splattered out too far, and they still fit.

How did we balance?

Were the muscles distributed differently then?

So now it will take a week of surreptitious mirror frontage practice to at least appear that the calf muscles see themselves as the legs' reliable saviour.

Second week is tango. Yes, some sultry, slinky passion—if we can remember what that was. I think we can remember steps from last week.

It's going so well. So maybe this is the exercise that will create repeat performances.

We provocatively hip wiggle around the room and then bend the thoracic vertebrae to curve and drape over co-senior's arm.

Then… something sticks, and we can't unstick.

Co-senior can't hold me up as he hasn't been to gym this week, and *thump*, we both land on the floor, giggling through our embarrassment as pantomaths stand over, resplendent in their superiority.

Well, steamed chilli, ginger, garlic whole barramundi tasted pretty good that day, even though we creaked to vertical and looked at the take-out menu on the wall for five minutes as we willed blood flow to the extremities so we could at least shuffle back to our car.

So, cycling…

Yes, I reckon that would be just perfect. I mean, didn't we all learn to ride when our brothers let go at the top of the hill and said peddle, brake, or die?

Again it was time to delve into the garage storage mould and find what used to be wonderful riding contraptions twenty years ago.

Of course, we were confident of staying upright. Co-senior rode for kilometres every weekend until I whined and bleated at the innumerable mobile-phone-user car drivers who lacked attention and saw a rider as an annoying inconvenience.

It was going to be a surreal moment riding around the lake, breathing in the air and feeding the ducks—an exercise excursion, healthy and so, so good for us.

Riding-a-bike skill never dies, but it can get a bit rusty. It took a few leg-over wobbles to remember the rhythm, and we were off. It does come back, but it doesn't all come back, as I shortly found out.

There were not meant to be people walking—wasn't this meant to be a bike track?

This myth was rapidly dumped as I veered into a Sunday-excursion family appearing 'round the corner. We all dominoed in fast succession in scintillating bursts, burying our bodies into flower beds and rain puddles.

So, off to the council swimming pool.

Yes, everyone said it worked wonders. No stiff, lovely people, cost effective.

And one, two, three, four, kick to the side, right left. Yes—I could do this.

I always imagined that I would be a ballerina jumping weightlessly through the air with legs in positions never experienced before.

I just wish the instructor would keep in time, maybe I can lend her my metronome. When you are a musician, these little off-beat moments can severely irritate.

And now we are forty-five minutes in, and my water retention problem is vigorously being sorted, but my bladder is also advising me that there has been a fluid relocation and an undercover leak could ensue and be identified by a stream of purple dye to make me die in embarrassment.

The steps out of the pool are tiny little wedges that only carry a foot sideways. How do I get out of the pool with sideways feet and pelvic muscles ready to explode?

How I wish I hadn't drunk eight glasses of water before midday.

I can't cough, I can't sneeze, just squeeze and run.

But now everything stings.

Have those pushy parents sent their little jewels to the pool every day for hours and hours and are their pelvic muscles under-developed and have they all peed in the pool and now I have a bacterial infection and there are bacteria spots on my arm?

No, co-senior, I don't want to swim anymore. It feels like germy haven.

Christie Brinkley is still, however, top of mind.

Maybe if I shut my eyes and just breathe deep, meditate, and relax, all will be revealed.

I lace up my runners, plug in the earbuds, tune into the latest iTunes playlist, and amble out the front door.

I notice spring blossoms are blooming to the left, wild bunnies are playing on the right, rainbow clouds are above my head and beautiful quotations are carved into the cement below my feet.

I am walking.

I am dreaming.

I am thinking.

I am breathing,

and I am living.

So, my thoughts, my lovelies—walk in the sand, and slide in the water.

Look left at the waves, look right at the sandcastle, look up at the blue sky, look down at the translucent water, and you will also dream and think and breathe and live.

It is all very simple, and it is right here in front of us.

Your soul will fly, and your cells will rejuvenate.

Your muscles will relax, and, Christie Brinkley—watch out I'm coming for ya.

HOMELESS

I JUMPED OUT OF BED THIS MORNING. WELL, MAYBE THAT is a slight exaggeration. I rolled over and pushed up and deep breathed and steadied myself and stood up. That's a better description.

Maybe it's more apt to say my mind jumped out of bed this morning.

A new day, a new beginning.

It was midwinter, my room was warm and cosy, my bed soft and feathery and never for one minute did it cross my mind that I was fortunate, so fortunate.

I dressed hurriedly in yesterday's leftovers strewn on the floor, threw on my woollies and jumped into the car to drop co-senior off at the local station. We were pretty proud of ourselves, as some kind Millennial had shown us how to top up the Opal card, and what usually proved to be an exceedingly costly exercise was not going to be much more than a tap. The 'old people's Opal' now is a benefit, and everyone is happy.

Co-senior alighted from train and exited station, brekkie in tum, cosy in coat, ready for the day. The sun rose slowly over the resource-rich east. Silhouetted in the sun's rays was the face of desolation—turning over, pushing up, deep breathing and steadying up from the impenetrable hard bed of a pavement.

A passerby reached down and handed this forlorn soul a hot cup of coffee and a sandwich. He cried and remarked to co-senior who was passing by that it could be his only meal today, and this morning had brought some compassion.

He remarked he couldn't hug her because PC had intercepted.

Co-senior opened his wallet and opened his arms and hugged hard.

Do we ever think of this as we lie in our ivory towers?

Do we know the stories of the bereft that cannot find their home?

Do we give even when we don't have?

Do we love as we should?

I was reading an article written by Rev Bill Crews from the Exodus Foundation, where he said:

> *Two dignified old homeless gents quietly queued for a meal in his Loaves and Fishes Free Restaurant. Curiously though, when they took their seats only one of them ate. The other patiently waited. As we watched this, we wondered what was going on. Why wasn't the other man eating? His meal was going cold. What happened next shocked us.*

> *When the first man finished his meal, he had a drink of water to clean his mouth. Then he took out his dentures and passed them to his mate who put them in and finally was able to enjoy his meal.*

> *These two homeless Australians were sharing one set of dentures.*

Rev Bill Crews was able to help, but brushing my teeth this morning, I was so grateful that I had them.

Do we think of this as we brush and floss and 'splintefy' in our beds to stop the first-world grinding?

Even from our privileged pedestals, we walk on countless occasions past the people who have nothing and need everything. These people hit hard times. People conveniently move on and hope the problem goes away. Young people take on the mantle of age and the musty of neglect. Razors and pads are so far out of reach, and survival is the only mantra.

It is just so damn sad.

We can all help in some way; researching how is just the beginning.

So, let's get started, Boomers.

We may be one of the fortunate so let's spray some of our fairy dust onto those who are not.

There is an element of guilt as I climb into my warm, fluffy, cosy bed, as the winter cold pervades, and I dream about the hell of homeless and am so very grateful for everything that I have.

I'M OFF TO LEARN KARATE

I GAVE SOMEONE THE FINGER TODAY. CAN A SENIOR SAY that?!

Well, it happened like this.

A young lady (am I allowed to say 'young lady', or is that PI?) Am I meant to say, 'young person', new driver? Oh, who cares, *young lady* it is to me.

So why are you, young lady, tailgating me in such an aggressive manner?

It is so damn dangerous.

Are you late for work? Have you missed your Tinder date? Has someone spilt Red Bull on your favourite singlet? Are you not wanting to reach my age?

Maybe you don't, 'cause it is looking pretty impossible right at this very moment. So, sharpen up and stop mucking with this senior citizen.

I will let you into a little secret. I am a master at Sudoku, and that means I am very logical. I have driven faultlessly for fifty years, so my anticipation and experience is spectacular. And one little add on—I'm rather more wily than you expect, young lady.

So this is my plan.

I am going to slow down, yes, really slow down to a snail's pace, and then I am going to slam on my brakes very fast, and if you don't take notice, you're surely going to get into trouble. That's OK if you smash my backside. It's your fault, and it would be a nasty reminder on your points system.

So while you are seething at my slow and steady and your veins are constricting and your blood pressure is not looking happy, I will tell you a little 'bedtime story' to calm you down, but don't you go to sleep.

My four-wheeled sturdy steed has got me out of real trouble in negotiating speedsters and swerving round right swipers at 100 kph. I know this rattly contraption is thirteen years old and is showing its age, but I love it 'cause the seats fit my bum. The new models dig into the home of my lymphatic gland system, and it means I have to step up my treatments.

Another little fact, oh entitled one, my thirteen-year-old skedonk nearly ended up out to trade-in pasture. It spent a very short time there, but Mumma came to the rescue.

I was very lucky that co-senior, after tsunami of tears, took my new car, a brand-spanking new addition to the family (purchased after trade-in), back to the car dealer. I was very lucky that he threw down the credit card and bought my well-worn beauty back. You see, I don't care about affluence or face or aging people movers. Our generation is very, very loyal, and it's way too early to neglect an aging family member.

But I do care about tailgating. So stop!

Well, back to karate.

I saw on the news today that road rage was now at extreme proportions. Who jumps out of their car and belts the living daylights out of a driver who tooted at them or wouldn't let them into their lane or gave them a finger?!

Ahhhh, note to myself — better not do that again.

Well sorry, it does happen, and there is vision on cam cars or car cams (not really sure what they are called), and it is ugly. Very, very ugly.

Better check my locks. Do they still central lock? Wouldn't have a clue—haven't locked my car for years.

And then, what do I do if someone barrels into my window to king-hit at the traffic lights? Do I recoil in rhythm? Do I level the new ring that hubby gave me for my sixty-fifth at eye level? I think I would think twice about that. That specific ring is too precious, and I wouldn't want to mangle the setting.

I could, however, close the window as fast as possible and drive off. Sorry, mate, your hand may be caught or even your head—now that would be gargoyley. It's not going to be a pretty sight when your hyperthyroid eyes pop out.

We could all just end up in a very messy halt.

So, back to karate.

I was in the city the other day. I was invisible. Well, maybe because I was wearing '*the uniform*'- the corporate uniform, black top, black bag, black skirt, black stockings, black shoes!

Cervical strain appears to be at its max, and while you are unawaredly glued to your screens, you may encounter a telephone pole or two, and a likely 'pole to nose smash' could just be the perfect accessory to the black.

I'm finding it fun to play 'Where's Wally' or my individual take on the game. It's 'Where's Red' or 'Where's Green'. It's a welcome distraction when you are smooshed into this little corporate ant swarm!

Us Boomerangers have an advantage, as we are unseen.

We listen for the little red man and charge and, at threat of annihilation, avoid any inadvertent bump. That angry glare burns through our inner core, and we are now too fragile for that. Everyone is so angry—la la la la la.

Now really, really back to karate.

I was walking beachside with co-senior. We were minding our own business and breathing in the freshness.

While recalling memories—the one's we could recall—we encountered an assembly of testosterone. Wasn't an issue, actually, until they started circling ominously. I was ready in *Hawaii 5-0* elite stance, back to back, hand up, ready for action.

One aggressor threw his hands in the air: 'High-5, codger! High-5, codger!'

We looked around. Who was the codger here? Aren't we still young 'uns? Didn't they know the difference?

Couldn't have been levelled at us, so we walked on with expletive admonishments from this rabble echoing across the waves.

So here is the thing. Our indifference may puzzle you, but listening to your taunts as we walk away will not work in your favour. You will be very surprised next time you try to take on this granny.

I will be very clear that I have had training.

My foundation is strong, and boy oh boy, it will be such an adventure.

I'm off to learn karate. And you may get a big surprise—I am ready for old age…

SILENCE
TO HEALING

─────────

I WAS FOUR.

I can remember the day like I had woken up to it this morning. I can hear the sounds. I can smell the smells. I am super alert.

It was zoo day, that special treat day when the vicissitudes of life had overwhelmed, and to avoid the challenges of child number three tipping the bucket, zoo day appeared on the calendar in the caring company of my mother's helper.

We laughed at the filter-free garbage spewed out by the colourful parrots. We laughed at the vulgarities plagiarised from errant visitors. We laughed at the sillies as we straddled the railing between birdcages. We just laughed.

I was four. It was fun, it was colourful, it was a beautiful day. So beautiful, we missed the beige spectre blurring the sideline. We missed the salivating predator; we missed the intention and choice of the course of action for the day.

It was just a lovely day.

Polar bears were even more exhilarating. Polar bear family was out in force, rumbling and tumbling and swimming, oblivious of their bareness and the gawking, passing parade—oblivious of the beige spectre standing at the side of the railing.

Contact was made with childlike coaxing, enticing and ensnaring. The back of the bear pit seemed like a wonderful place to really engage with the magnificent white beasts—no need for the helper to join in; maybe better to look after the four-year- old's belongings in the visitor viewing below.

I remember like it was this morning. I was four. I remember the scrape of the zipper, I remember the engorged weapon, I remember the boring, expectant eyes, I remember the grab of my wrist... and I remember the sound of the steps of the helper coming 'round the corner. I remember it all. I was the lucky one.

I was twelve and on a bus adventure into the city for an amalgam onslaught with the promise of high tea at Stuttafords (this was Johannesburg) as bribe for good behaviour. Sugar after a filling—go figure!

Drills attached to aluminum hoses invaded the cavity, but not as invasive as the dental mirror shoved down the top of a twelve-year-old girl and rubbed vigorously against the nipples hiding in the 'first bra' protection.

Oh yeah, remember it like it was today.

Those were those days. We just didn't talk about it.

Myriads of situations osmosis'd into our subconscious and hid surreptitiously in decades of memory. It was just expected to be stiff upper lipped, stoic in the face of adversity.

It was almost dishonourable to speak about failures or challenges or abuse, and never anything ever broached below the belt.

Our emotions were taught to be repressed and emotionally stunted, going right back to centuries of British ancestry and challenges in times of war. (Still love you like crazy, my beautiful Brit blood brothers).

Thank goodness for now—we have help everywhere. We are taught to reach out and talk out and visit therapists and go online and share and join likewise groups and face our hurts to achieve our healing.

Even Prince Harry had the guts to open the gates of healing.

We all have problems. The freedom is in acknowledging them, seeking help and trusting our families to listen and never let it happen again.

It's now the time to move from Silence to Healing.

I'M TRUE TO MYSELF AND THAT MAKES ME BEAUTIFUL

CHUCK THE 'I FEEL GUILTY'. DON'T WE HEAR IT ALL THE TIME?

Guilty I didn't look after elderly parents.

Guilty that I burned the pizza.

Guilty that I screamed at my kid for spilling petrol from the petrol siphon over my shoes (maybe a little less guilty on this one, as they were my favourite shoes).

Guilty that I gave the grandbaby too much sugar.

Guilty that I divorced and unsettled the family status quo.

Guilty that I left someone out unknowingly.

Guilty that I called my husband a workaholic.

Guilty that I didn't disturb those who made me too hard to love.

Guilty that I stuffed my kids with florentines when we emigrated, while we all got fat.

Guilty that I promised a dinner party, and it never happened.

Guilty that I drank milk straight out of the bottle.

Guilty that I didn't say goodbye to my friend and told him I loved him before he died.

Guilty that my Facebook profile is at twenty years old.

And on, and on, and on.

Chuck the guilty, beautifuls.

'Punch a hole through perfection, it's simply a myth.' (So said a quote I read but can't remember where.)

Be real, not perfect. It makes you SO BEAUTIFUL.

LOOKING
AFTER MUM

———

THE PHONE CALL I RECEIVED TODAY MADE ME CRY. REALLY cry.

My mum was found in the bath after lying there overnight. She was glazed and shaken, suffering from hypothermia and oh so vulnerable in her nudity after lying there overnight.

I was so grateful that she was at least robust, strong, and feisty and a brave 'resister', as otherwise she most certainly would not have made it.

She was 82!

She had lain in her bath, as was her usual custom, regurgitating the day to herself. Her bath was her relaxing haven, her abode of snugness.

On trying to stand up, her arthritic knee had buckled, preventing her from rising. There was no emergency button or adjacent neighbours, and she lay for twelve hours with oxygen and carbon dioxide relaying through the night. It was only daylight that brought respite, and embarrassment was enveloped by survival.

And then the time she fell into the garden bed, hallucinating amongst variegated beds of vegetation. No one saw her, no one heard her. It was a perfect hidey-hole from an ugly world. Her voice was a bleat, her ankle contorted, and her dignity departed.

Poor Mum — always so dignified, and now the aridness of age slowly taking her back to her origin.

I now lived in another country, whilst my sister and brother were left to manage the many challenges. How exhausting it must have been for them on a daily basis, especially when old age became irrational and brittle. They came through with many struggles but many successes.

All this fueled the guilt of separation. Separated by oceans but still right alongside. The phone was our auditory saviour. No Facetime in those days, as her face bore into my soul from the tiny picture frame next to my computer and was absorbed like an osmotic drug.

The news of her death made me howl like a primal animal, and oh, how I wish I could have told her in person one more time that I loved her and not utter these words to her recorded answering machine message.

She would have been one hundred this year and is long gone.

And now, as seniors we face the other side, and I ask fellow seniors, What have we all learned, and what is still to learn?

Did we interfere, or were we simply concerned?

Did we enter a personal turf that was being defended mightily?

Were we well intentioned or just interfering?

Did we bitch too hard about the fatigue and responsibility and guilt?

Did we engage rather than assess?

Were we well intentioned with our suggestions for her wellbeing?

OK, from our perspective. Now, to our children...

I know that co-senior and I would cling desperately to our independence. In fact, we would be fierce in this pursuit.

We would always know that you were just there, just a phone call away, should we encounter difficulty and need your unconditional help.

We would want you to care *about* us and not care *for* us.

We would want you to visit and talk and laugh and make memories, not check to see that we had remembered to put the chicken back in the fridge or were eating the out-of-date hummus.

Don't make us defensive or stubborn. We are not resisting; we are just holding on to our sense of worth and some control of our dignity. We are cognizant that life and time seem to be trickling away.

Doesn't make us feel like seniors.

Doesn't make us behave like seniors.

Doesn't make us think like seniors.

Doesn't make us do like seniors.

Getting old is, oh, so comfortable.

Now, there is no peer pressure, and we can be as immature as we feel.

We are simply unstoppable—if we only could get started!

SHARED ECONOMIES

So, WHAT DO YOU DO WHEN YOUR CORPORATE LIVES END?

Do you sink into a very deep, dark, long depression?

Do you step up your volunteering with the grey brigade searching for more purpose in life?

Do you become number one unpaid grandparent on call every minute for daily babysitting?

Or do you remain relevant and go out there and see what pushes the button to jump out of bed and say, 'Whoopee! It's another glorious day'?

Don't get me wrong, volunteering and grandparenting is uber, uber relevant—but does it contribute to the capitulation of winding down till the munitions of the brain and body just *stop*?

I don't know—help me out here!

When the corporate life ends, its sucks and shocks and relieves and innovates.

Co-senior and I, for instance, have been in the workforce all our lives. We learned our skills in corporations and then evolved into the entrepreneurial space.

Nothing is more exhilarating than brainstorming and having the guts to go for it. There are no losers here, just those who are willing to freely take a chance and not collapse if failure is part of the process.

Certain personalities hate failure. It makes them sad. They communicate with 'all good' face, even when they are collapsed and down on their knees.

Why do we fear to fail? Nobody cares really.

Cher once expressed, 'If it doesn't matter in five years, then it doesn't matter', so don't spend five minutes on it.

For the past twenty-five years, our work life had been illuminated in magical fairground lights, eating cheese sticks and fairy floss and throwing balls into clown appendages. 'Wake me up', I would say, 'is this my workspace? How lucky am I?'

However, travelling and managing and lifting and organising took its toll, and we shut shop abruptly after the disappointment of human behaviour in a sale negotiation.

We knew it was time, but—boom!—life was now different.

So, what now?

Of course, the thought of a year's sabbatical exploring hidden temples and cultures and wildlife is a bit titillating, but it almost feels guilty thinking about it after the conditioning of daily work life and responsibilities.

It just feels like there is still just that little bit more to squeeze out. Not until there is 'nothing left, discarded', squeezed out. No, the deep discovery that there is still just that little bit more to create and innovate.

So then it is the road to exploration, and it exposes quite a varied path.

Uber driving seems to be a perfect part-time day for lonely seniors, and from what I hear, they just love it. Some have lost businesses, some have lost partners, some are losing their minds in boredom, and some want to just take back control of their lives, clicking in and out when their timing prefers.

They have crossed the divide of loneliness. They chatter from pick up to pick up, share life experiences if wanted, mix with corporate execs and hen night party girls and then switch off the light knowing that they have had a day of relevance.

Part-time mystery shoppers are having fun.

No need to be lonely.

There are cars to drive and meals to enjoy and clothes to try and bad-attitude shop attendants to 'out'. Senior sleuth specialist — now that's a new job title!

Now we can become owner vehicle, courier services.

We tried this one for a while, and a few emojis would superbly typify this eye-opening experience.

Well, it's not hard, it's simply unexpected.

I mean, if you are a major corporate and need a parcel to be delivered 'chop smart' to another major corporate, your expectations of a senior couple with branded caps and bright eyes and bushy tails arriving at your premises, trolley in tow, is mind-altering.

Bright and breezy 'can do' attitude leaves a stunning impression, and as we high viz out of the building humming, 'This is the best day of my life', stunned execs in full hypnosis open their app to give a rather confused five-star rating.

There is only one small problem — we live in the burbs, and what is going on with the elevators in the centre city high rises? There are no buttons. How do you get up and down, and how do you get out if you have a claustrophobic moment, encased in steel? Is it that long since we have journeyed into the big smoke?

OK, so now I see an iPad at the end. Do we press the floor number? And what happens if I change my mind? Who will come and get me — I could be on the fifty-sixth floor?!

Then, I have to take a picture of my delivery, but my camera on my phone in the app won't work, and I don't understand why? I'll just have to take a photo and store it on my phone and then work out how to send it on to whomever I should be sending it on to.

Not so easy, huh?

But I ran something past co-senior, that maybe we could accept an assignment that commenced at 1.30 a.m. with delivery by 3 a.m. It was only intercity to the suburbs, and this one was for the big 'biccies'.

Just one movement, and job done for the week. Is it because of an urgent job or precious container or have-to-get-there-on-time deadline?

Haven't a clue!

But can you imagine the faces as two co-seniors arrive at the seedy nightclub for pick up? 'Hello there, we are your friendly senior couriers at your service. We can do, we are willing, we are responsible.'

Then the thought occurred—*What if we were transporting a little white powder to the burbs and knew nothing about the contents of the package?* Co-senior is very practical and saw that this one just could be fraught with danger, so the little jobs remained safely on the roster.

Then, of course, we can share peer to peer, share our cars, share our homes, and share our stuff. We can all have a share of the pie, and everyone is happy.

Endless possibilities are out there—some inspiring and some just hard work, but it's good to explore all these new 'innovative economies'. It may quite simply keep us alive.

PUSHED INTO IRRELEVANCE— IDENTITY AND HOPE

COLIN POWELL, A FOUR-STAR GENERAL IN THE US ARMY, had a career filled with honour and intrigue. He was powerful in the true sense one day and under the sink the next, fixing the plumbing and flopping around in his empty space.

He was used to giving orders. Now he's submitting to orders from 'Commander in Chief' at home.

How did he feel?

Was he present in this space, or was he nervous and anxious?

Did he feel irrelevant and lost or creative and free?

I know that, from my side of the coin, closing our business was a big shock. We employed many people, we were used to making decisions for ourselves and for others and we worked hard at keeping abreast of technology and the transformation from traditional marketing to the data driven form—now a university course in itself.

What we had learned at university was becoming fast irrelevant, while even the 'business speak' was for us unusual and unfamiliar.

Disrupters have made many businesses sharpen their tools, and in many ways, this is wonderful. They are the brave entrepreneurs with an innovation mindset creating a new market while disrupting what exists. Market leaders in different industries and in existing markets are rapidly being displaced. The change is rapid, and we Boomers who are comfortable with our business methodology have to adapt and learn fast and furious to have any kind of relevance in this new world. And this sometimes can take away our mojo as we struggle to keep up.

Sometimes we frantically seek as much information as our brains can absorb. And sometimes, we don't care, as we know deep inside that we will never be as astute as our juniors in the new fields of business.

The skills for today were learned way back in their youth and are their derivative of reading, writing and arithmetic. It's their new code of learning.

Isn't this obvious when we ask our grandchild to repair our computer's DNA, when we have confidently realized that it is all just logic (but find our logic these days is slightly impaired)?

We can either be dinosaurs and throw in the towel, remaining in the old world of knowledge and comfort. We can spin out of control and into heart attacks and high blood pressure trying to understand the new language of today, or we can merrily jog along with a foot in both camps, not caring that we are not perfect but giving it a go anyway.

We are losing our identity at a rapid pace, and we don't have the energy to re-instate in this new world way of life. So, we learn self-checkout at the supermarket, online ordering of Groupon sales items, settings and data and Bluetooth and apps. We trade on Gumtree and eBay and Ziilch and Sell My Car—this, of course, in the process of minimalizing.

Or maybe we are all justifying this new look, when really enjoying the 'time to play' money that dribbles in. This gives us hope when we feel that we have no place in this disparate, fast-changing world. If we don't give it a try, we are only feeding our despair that we are not able to exist in this new, changing world.

Hope is our gift from the mind, and it is now compelling us to act.

Our family members may think we are just getting old and empathize with us and each other as they wink behind our backs. But now is the time, Boomers.

It is time for us to be disrupters.

We need to disrupt the new generation's impression of us.

We need to be our own people.

We all feel the same, but let's get out there and shake up our demographic. We won't be pushed into irrelevance.

We had identities then and even more so now, and if we stick to the plan, we will always life-changingly hold on to hope.

DON'T GIVE UP WHEN OTHERS DO IT BETTER

WELL, I GOT LUCKY.

I have a daughter-in-law who is a *MasterChef* contender, a daughter with a beautiful singing voice, a sister who paints like Picasso, and to top it all, a Greek friend (everyone needs to have a Greek friend) who puts me into anxiety spin when we all get together and it's my turn to cook.

Let's backtrack a little.

My forte is an ice bowl—a beautiful symmetrical receptacle for homemade lemon ice cream. Seasonal flowers are beautifully encased in the layers of ice, and appreciative 'aahs' always follow the presentation.

The technique is learned from a gourmet chef, and methodology is carefully guarded.

Don't we all do that? Don't we protect our little piece of uniqueness?

I am a good cook. I have entertained bounteously. The daily grind of everyday is varied and tasty, and I have even evolved into toddler delights with their little preferences.

So why, then, the weeks of planning if anyone comes over?

Why does the oven not seem to stay true to temperature?

Why do our recipes lack expression, and current ingredients sound so futuristic?

Why does it sometimes lead to a tiny bit of misrepresentation and horror when a friend asks for a recipe and wants to eyeball the serrated spring pan used when we are fully aware that the apple tart had been hastily purchased from the nearest bakery when the pavlova had collapsed and crumbled? Funny how the pan miraculously disappears.

We seniors used to cook differently.

Firstly, traditions led to sit-down family meals. And in our days (one should never say that; it dates us) it was the body nourishing spag bol, chicken pie, veal schnitzel, fish and chips, and the ultimate lamb roast with all the trimmings. Those were in my household, but may have been considerably different in yours.

We thought this was balanced. We thought we were really progressive when melted Ghee was not the first step. We got that that was even a generation before us and was nutritionally clogging our hearts. We didn't notice our little cherubs getting larger and larger. It was a symbol of prosperity and wealth. We hadn't heard—or chose not to hear—about vegan, gluten free, keto, low carb. Different generation, different traditions, and different knowledge. But we still cooked damn well.

Now food is an art.

It is so beautiful that it takes prominence on socials. It is quite illuminating. I know what everyone in my circle has eaten for the past month. No wonder they are shrinking—sprout of a spring onion, smear of avocado, and a scallop is doing the trick. Gives some ideas, but I'm not even going to attempt working with certain ingredients. I can't pronounce or spell them, so not sure if they are spit from an Amazon piranha or cane toad sperm, and I'd have to do a whole origin searching exercise before I can even describe them. I mean, have you ever heard of gochujang, wakame, or ugli fruit? Well, there you go; neither have I.

Then there is my Greek friend. Why does everything she produces taste like gold? It's so morish and effortless and abundant—it feels like an abyss between her offerings and mine. We live in the same climate, and there are no harsher conditions at our home. The variety of ingredients are the same, we don't boil our vegies, we use lots of herbs—but it's not the same.

First reaction is not to invite our acquired family round to the house or subtly hint at 'bring a plate' to be integrated between our straitlaced offerings.

Are we going to give up and just see them less?

And then there is the family member who is so talented—follows the family genes and paints like a snapshot.

Where does one learn that? Is it genetic?

My only offering on a huge canvas that loudly hung in our sitting room was so out of proportion—and can I say, 'unique'—that guest's pretence of non-awareness gave them an opportunity to stifle their giggles? Or, when accosted by the gargantuan nonconforming canvas, practiced a skilled exercise in 'shlunking' down to protect any awareness of deceit.

Are we going to give up because we don't conform to the way art should look?

And the pièce de résistance? I used to be a rock chick. I sang in a band. I won a prestigious vocal award. I am classically trained. I play the guitar. I released vinyls. I was contracted to a record company for ten years….. Not trying to brag here, just making a point.

I produced a beautiful human being with a beautiful voice who released albums and performed all over the world, and I stepped back. My voice dissolved into sotto voce. Muscles weakened, guitar gathered dust, and I just became ordinary.

And then I woke up.

This life is not a competition, seniors. Our times may have been different, and it's all moving so fast.

But, if we were fine cooks, we are still very fine cooks.

If we paint in our way, we are our own Van Gogh. It's not right or wrong, it's perfect, and it's time to sing and belt out loud, strapped to our guitars.

No one is better than us. They are simply different, and that difference is loudly celebrated. Go out and roar significant, seniors. Never give up.

We all have our own specialness and will be applauded loudly for always having a go.

'Apathy masquerades itself as humility, and there is nothing humble about living an apathetic life.' – Erwin MacManus

TODAY I AM
DOING NOTHING

—

GOOD MORNING.

My neurons are regrouping.
My neurons are receiving nourishment.
My neurons are being recalibrated.

Good night.

STUCK IN THE
MIDDLE WITH YOU

———

OUR OWN BUSINESS HAS BEEN A BIG PART OF OUR LIVES.
It was relevant business and successful business. We learned how
to lead and inspire and worked damn hard.

It was busy and rewarding and challenging and exciting.

And then it…

STOPS.

It feels like the head has been dismembered from the body
while the legs are continuing to run, flailing around in identity
confusion.

We knew that our brand of business would evolve fast, and at
this stage in life, we knew it would be a challenge to keep up.

Businesses everywhere were being affected by shared economies and digital disruption, and we didn't want to be pulled into
this vortex to be spat out unsuccessfully on the other side.

Industries were changing—video rental businesses, travel services, taxi services, and more. The big ONLINE was now the go.
We had to give it a try or vanish into prehistoric methods of sales
that were no longer working effectively.

We are 'stuck in the middle'—stuck between Millennial and Dinosaur.

Running our own business was firmly imprinted in our DNA. We smartly surrounded ourselves with Gen X,Y, and Zs.- (Why didn't we just follow the Google trend and call it Gen Alphabet?) The challenge is that we don't quite know when one Gen starts and when one Gen ends. It's a bit like the horoscope signs—Gen Aquarius, Gen Pisces…

Being very busy, active Boomer business owners, here lies another problem. We are so engrained in the old world. Not *old* as in old, grey, worn, forgetful. No, *old* as in style and methods and verbalizing and face-to-face meetings and twenty-five- plus years services with gold watches as gifts on retirement.

Actually, that is not absolutely true, as our doctor of thirty-five years, on retirement, quietly walked out of his office on the last day without any hoohah, never to be seen again.

So, now we have one foot in the Jurassic period and one foot in the digital movement. And we must work fast, very fast to keep up, and this goes against everything going on in our bodies and brains at this stage in our lives.

We were doing very nicely, thank you, when it was just one world, but now that we have a foot in both worlds, the stretch hurts!!

Our dinosaur family warms and feeds the soul. This is not business now but day-to-day life. We entertain at home and laugh and call and 'coffee catch up' together.

We debate about the issues of the world around cups of tea and glasses of wine and 'bring your own plate'.

We moan about the 'now'—probably sour grapes as we don't fully understand the social movements of today. We ensure that local community issues are addressed by our councils and debate about who in our community is graffiti'ing our parks or damaging our vehicles at shopping centres.

We are learning that the meaning of LOL, which to us is 'lots of love', means 'laugh out loud'.

FOMO sounds like a new washing powder that lathers up well. DM is deep and meaningful. And 'Poke' me?!

Now there is a whole new vocabulary that we need to learn.

And what's with the communication on the 'device' across the restaurant table rather than communication with each other?

The finger has become the voice. Phones flirt and talk with each other, and we question why we are even there.

Our choice is to work in one world or the other.

If we don't graduate and evolve into the new world, we will become oh so boring and so one dimensional. We will be an unshielded twisted pair over the 'unshielded twisted pair' (internet terminology, by the way).

Bridging this gap isn't fun.

We don't understand each other, but we are willing to try.

We will succumb and let you rule, but don't make us irrelevant in the process.

And while we are evolving, we will also sit around the table with our besties, drinking red wine, shooting the shit, solving the world's issues, and still talking, sharing, and laughing.

HELL, BABY, I'M GLAD I'M STUCK IN THE MIDDLE WITH YOU!

SENIOR MOMENTS

I KNOW HIS NAME.

I know I know his name.

I know every mark on his face and every hair out of place. I can even recite his lines in *Top Gun*, but WHAT THE HELL IS HIS NAME?

A knowing glance passes between co-senior and I — the knowing glance that says, 'Is this some serious health issue or only a temporary brain freeze?'

We set our stopwatches and go…

If we get it in five minutes, then everything is A-OK. We flip-flop through the alphabet, egging each other on, shaking each other's marbles, working fast and furious against the clock.

Ping!!!

It's Tom. But surname? Craft, Crud, Crude… Got it! Boom — it's Cruise!

We crack a bottle of champagne in celebration.

My mum used to say the memory works well with paired association. It worked very well for her until she called Mrs Rind Mrs Bacon at an upmarket Medical Association convention. Despite this social embarrassment, I thought I would practice it in my repertoire.

But it wasn't that pretty when Jane Crapp walked up to me at a school function and I confidently introduced her to my circle of friends as Jane Poo. And where do you go from there? Run to the carpark, I would say—fast, very fast, and get out of there.

Talking about carparks.

Are cars getting bigger, or are we getting smaller?

Why is the carpark like a labyrinth in our consciousness and a trap for forgetful seniors wandering between floors trying to remember the colour and level of their hidden vehicle?

We do remember, actually, but write it down on the hairdresser receipt that was filed in the handbag's safe place amongst old lipsticks, breath fresheners, hairbands, pens, and loose coin.

My local carpark is very familiar, until some smartass planner decided to paint the arrows in all different directions to 'correct' the flow of impatient parkers. It resulted in just the opposite, with abuse being hurled out of windows at unfamiliar drivers driving in the wrong direction and the jiggy jiggy quickstep of manoeuvring the behemoths around each other to evacuate.

This is, however, my carpark. I stop here at least once a week for groceries and coffees, so I know it well. I don't have to be Christopher Columbus on a voyage of discovery to find my little grey automobile.

But today, I just can't find it.

It has definitely been stolen.

My heart breaks and skips at the same time as it really is time for a new car, but I would never forgive myself if I didn't say goodbye in a proper and loving manner—even if multiple door bumps had given this little voomer a bad case of acne.

I know that I had absolutely, conclusively left the car in my usual spot.

So now it's been stolen.

Terror settles in as I try to recall what I had left in the car over the past year. I don't care if the perpetrator catches some mouldy virus. They deserve it, actually.

But I think I left my to-do list on the front seat, and now I don't have a clue of what there is to do for the rest of the day and month and the rest of my life. I am a very strong list maker, and my life is in the list.

And I banked today. Did I leave my banking details on the to-do list?

So now my car is gone *and* my to-do list *and* my life savings. Things are getting better every minute—not!!!

And last but not least, I borrowed my friend's favourite dress, and it is gone, and so is the friendship, I would say.

In my enormous distress, peering through anguished tears, I see my little silver steed settled in the abyss between two mammoth SUVs. Its little bent number plate peaks tentatively between the gaps.

You go, girl—you will be found.

I am not so sure that everything needs to be found.

Occasional cleaners, thank goodness, have been written into our budget. We just can't get to the under couch 'nooks and crannies' these days. And, if we do, it's a whole procedure to get back up again.

I am always very joyful when cleaning day comes around.

Problem is, though, that there always needs to be a cleanup before the cleaners clean up. We worked out that it was all just a wasteful occurrence if the carpet didn't fully present, corner to corner, or the counters couldn't be seen in their full glory.

There are some things, however, that need not be seen in their full glory.

Co-senior's job is to empty the bins prior to the arrival of these angel workers. I don't feel comfortable with any home intruders delving through the personal items that are freely dumped in the bin on the other twenty-seven days.

Sometimes it becomes a hurried job to empty the bin before the knock on the door, and co-senior would frantically grab the contents of the bin and place in his T-shirt drawer to deal with at a later stage.

This plan was working gloriously, but sometimes senior moments change the path.

Co-senior waved goodbye to go to the local cafe to purchase the newspapers. Life and routine were running ever so smoothly. He returned home, flung the newspapers on the table, and turned around to collect his coffee, and stuck to his back in mirthful surrender was a white, flapping, sticky Tena pad. He had only just remarked that everyone was smiling at him today, and nobody said a thing!

Talking about pads, this was the finish line for our little terrier. He became our nappy baby as he stared vacantly out of the window in his eighteenth year, not able to arrest the flow from his digestive system.

Co-senior and I were so very sad when he left us, but if we were going to empty nest, better to empty nest the children and the dog at the same time.

Co-senior's friend is having a senior moment and is irked as he has been left 'babysitting' the damn dog. He never wanted a dog in this later stage of life, but his children thought differently, and cootchy, cootchy, brought home a dog-pound adoptee.

And now everyone has left the nest. His wife is working on the other side of town. His children are never home, and he is left discussing his problems with his doe-eyed companion. This dog is not a good listener and would much rather spend his time trying to 'houdini' off the balcony or bolt across the major highway if an eentsy crack of the door was left ajar in a senior moment.

In fact, talking about that, another friend had a serious senior moment when their three-year-old granddaughter was found skipping down the pavement a kilometre away, only to be found just in time before the parents arrived for pick up. They rapidly purchased a child pen to keep the chillies encased. We passed on this information to our intrepid dog babysitter, who has now found the playpen-prison solution very effective, and he can now follow his path of freedom and read his *Economist*, if he can only find his glasses.

So, I have left my glasses on a table, my keys on the toilet, my bag on the counter, my purse in the shop, my credit card in the machine, my watch at the gym, and my brain at home.

Apparently, the solution is the Tile — one of those fancy new-age tracking devices. How does it work and where do you put it? What use is it going to be if it is attached to the keys that are cuddling with the other keys in 'lost property'?

There is now a plan SLB — STOP, LOOK, BACK.

I promise, if you do that, your stuff will make it home with you.

I made delicious poached eggs this morning. They rested on smashed avocado and feta cheese. I understand that this is a thing at the moment.

I tried to do sudoku and aborted after too many duplications.

I sped out the door, as I was late for an appointment, and I must admit I applied my lipstick in the car, missed the edges, and now looked like a comic performer.

After travelling for 10 kilometres, I screamed to a halt. Did I switch the oven off?

I reroute the GPS and circle back home, only to see a cloud of smoke permeating the sky in the direction of home. A wailing fire engine screams past in the same direction. My brain screams, *It's my house!*

I enter the street — all is quiet on the home front.

No, I may have senior moments, but I am not moving into the retirement village — no, not just yet.

IT'S LONELY
BEING ONELY

SOME OF US HAVE PARTNERS THAT ARE NO LONGER HERE.
Some of us have never had partners.
Some of us don't want to be with the partners we have anymore.
Some of us wish just to have a partner.
Some of us are suffocating in our loneliness.
I hear about this pain over cups of coffee.

My singles tell me that the twilight refuses to end, and the lonely weight that constantly pervades settles in between the heart and the head.

It seems that the darkest hour is at the end of the day. This is the time that spirited, exhausted families regroup.

And yet, for my singles, their only friend is a blank wall, a staccato television, a dog-eared book (with eyes too tired to absorb), and the urge to scream at the nothing. All this while they endeavour to shut down the gates of pain so they no longer hurt or translate into the worthlessness of depression.

They vocalize hard to themselves and then pour another alcoholic beverage, washed down with a mind-numbing sleeping tablet.

Observing this season of aloneness makes me hug my co-senior, cherish my co-senior and respect the precious time we have been given.

The aloneness for all does not similarly evolve.

My family suffered and suffers this void.

My mum had so many dreams, so many adventures, so many plans — stolen away by patriarch's Parkinson's, an insidious, progressive, debilitating, and heartbreaking disease. Parkinson's made her angry and cheated, and only the comfort of two scotches every night soothed the emptiness.

She would tell me about the 'witching' hour. For us, this hour used to be manic and frustrating as we coerced little family members to climb into bed and fall asleep. For her, this messiness would have infiltrated the echo of silence with joy, and the feeling of belonging would have been tangible.

How I wish that I had listened longer and more often to her war stories and love stories and indelible memories of times that still remained in her consciousness. The phone became her companion, breaking the distance across the miles and the curse of loneliness.

I asked my sister about her end of the day. She had converted this space into Conversations with God. Good on you, I say, just let us make friends with your friend our own way. Friendships are differently formed and create their own individual depth in an individual manner.

Friend One, who woke up to a dead husband lying next to her in bed sent waves of shock through the friendship community. He was a healthy man, even competing for his country.

He was omnipotent and strong and rosy-cheeked, never considering that he would run out of family and friends and time. Autolysis commenced, protein filaments locked, muscles became rigid, and joints stiffened, and he was gone, leaving behind a sea of heartbreak. My friend's loneliness was tangible, heartbreaking, unforgiving, vacant, and suicidal. It felt like she would never be able to peek over to the other side. She suffocated in the evening hour, stifled by loneliness, despair, and red wine.

As a friend, it was time to step up through personal melee and share a voice, just a voice, till weariness enveloped and soothed.

I am happy to say that this friend has slowly taken a few steps up the ladder of life and has tentatively placed her leg on the other side. She is wearing a protective helmet, but guess what? If she falls, we have a friendship safety net right in place and are ready and able to catch her.

Friend Two's husband disintegrated into an unconscious mess as he hit a barrier wall at high speed. Not only did his body disintegrate, but his brain was also shattered into little fragments. He was doing what he loved, if that was the only consolation. He was free and fearless and fulfilled. Friend Two moved on fast. She would not submit to loneliness and married his racing partner. This was in pretty quick succession, and I wondered if while they toasted his ashes on the mantelpiece, he blew back little filaments of calcium phosphate trying to generate a little choke reflex in his absence.

We are all so different. Hers was not a lonely hour; maybe just a lonely half hour.

Friend Three's ninety-three-year-old husband left her last year for another woman. This one seems a tad suspicious. I mean, ninety-three years old! It couldn't have been the rabid coupling that spurred him on or his chiselled body that stirred her on. Maybe it was his wicked mind and libidinous eyes.

Or, getting to the nitty-gritty, maybe he was tailored by success and his bank balance had something to do with it.

This friend took it in her stride.

Of course, she still had her lonely hour, but she has far too much going on that it never leeched into insecurities. She was now free — no more chauffeuring and walking frames and denture breath of lingering bacteria. She was off on a flight to anywhere interesting, absorbing her love of history and exploration.

And then my cancer widow survivor friend. She is the friend who has spent years watching her love fade and shrink and fight and hope and die. She is a colourful friend—a bright pink lady, an aureate yellow lady whose aura was starting to fade ever so slowly to beige.

Her lonely hour seeped into every fragment of her inner soul. Tears consumed her, and the threat of becoming nondescript without her bowerbird was about to become her evolution.

She yelled and cried and stiffened her lip. She was an old-school stoic, always with a face of 'I'm all right', but dripping blood under the skin.

I see you, my friends.

I see you leave the room when it feels too much and your breath won't catch up with your breathing.

I know that your firm exterior is mashed banana inside.

I know that your lonely hour is plain painful.

But I look around and know that with time the pain will pass.

Your spring is around the corner.

I see the start of colour in your necklace today. Soon that colour will be bold, and your past will be gently pushing you into your future, unseen but not forgotten.

I speak above to my girlie Boomers, but my 'boysie' Boomers grieve more quietly. In their indescribable pain and loneliness, they don't talk.

Some slide into oblivion.

Some sink their sorrows in flagons of ale.

Some join 'sheds' when they have no interest or skill in carpentry. They are there solely to commune if they can.

Some metamorph into *Rocky* or try to, although in actual fact, a personal trainer told me there is not much muscle growth after seventy-three. Hope this is not in all departmentals!

These singles flock to the inexperienced, who gird them on to open their wallets and preen at their conquests.

I am watching one of my bestie 'boysie' baby Boomers. I am watching him — he watches me but doesn't see.

I listen to his stories — same story every ten minutes. For him, it is wonderful to tell the tale for the first time. I can now repeat it verbatim.

I wonder if he experiences his lonely hour?

Is his brain feeling lonely, or does he always see home wherever he is? I would say he is blessed.

For him, I am his mother, his sister, his friend, his daughter, his mother, his sister, his friend, his daughter. Co-senior is also his mother, his sister, his friend, his daughter.

There is always someone there to tell his story to every ten minutes.

He is drowning in his amnesia, but for him, life is sublime, and it will never, ever be lonely being 'onely'.

A WEE LITTLE PROBLEM

CO-SENIOR WOKE UP IN A COLD SWEAT THIS MORNING.

The next minute, he was buried in the folds of a rising doona — he had disappeared and was now closely mimicking Casper the ghost.

Obviously, something very strange was going on here. Maybe I had misinterpreted and he was having a hot flush, not a cold sweat. Maybe the doona was giving him ultimate cooling aeration.

I dug my head under the doona as well to keep his anxiety company.

He told me he had had a nightmare.

I am sure we all have nightmares now and then, demographic specific nightmares…

The grandbaby has fallen into the pool on our shift.

The kids have separated and moved back in with the whole 'enchilada'.

Everything benign is now cancerous.

We can't remember our words and are about to walk on stage, and nobody can find the script for prompting.

And, at last, we can fly as we flap our wings, but we are falling, falling, falling off a tower that touches the sky.

All our bits have fallen off.

Well, the nightmare actually was about bits, and he admitted to me that he was pretty relieved that all the bits were 'present and correct'.

I did have a little giggle seeing his distress and relief, but I understand it all better now as he settled in to recount his imaginative slumber. So here goes...

Co-senior had zillions of meetings today.

It was an all-over-town, in-obscure-places kind of day, and the day went well.

Business was good, coffee was drunk, and three litres of water consumed. Isn't that the prescription for healthy blood flow to a sane brain?

The trip home was enjoyable with Ted Talks, light music, signed contracts, and a promise of date night on return.

The city is growing, and infrastructure is bursting at the seams. Roadworks jump up to bite. Lollipop signs spring up in the hands of backpackers shifting from foot to foot to stop the endless tedium and instigate the slow staccato for the journey home. The creeping pace is stifling.

And then a wee little problem arises.

Where does all the fluid go? Three litres into a kidney bean doesn't fit—it overflows—now what? Need to pee, where to pee? Can't stop to pee, all I can think about is pee. I think I may need to wear a pee pad—I'm now in trouble pee!

The Berocca-filled plastic bottle for co-senior is now looking very attractive—he hates plastic but couldn't find the drink flask this morning.

Traffic upfront is at a standstill as the trucking world works overtime, coordinating axles side by side. Single cars make their way around obstructions, but nooo, nobody is going to let a Merc in—senior in Merc, even worse—as frustrated drivers grab control with a snarl of comeuppance.

Co-senior is stuck.

So, there are options. Let rip and face the consequences: experience a renal rupture—that wouldn't be good, and would have to cancel date night—or tip the Berocca slowly out of the door, release the joystick, and boom into the bottle.

OK, that is doable, but there's no place to go undercover—jackets are not trending in office wear, and as a senior, one has to keep current.

Action now needs to be as swift as Ivan Origone on a good day.

And will co-senior lose points? Mobile phone use annihilates half your licence these days. So, what is the consequence of a plonker pee—surely it couldn't be the same?

This is a delicate, very sophisticated piece of apparatus. Could it be the whole 'lose all points and licence for the year' scenario?

'I promise you, officer, it is mobile, it is a device, but it's not talking!'

Hey, presto, zip down, bottle mouth open, sausage positioned—relief.

Speedy response is needed now as traffic is moving and P-plater is letting Merc merge. That's a first.

Holy shit, the baloney pony is stuck—and P-plater is smiling and waving and blood flow is stopping and traffic is moving and this is a very awkward situation. Zipper rips up, plonker and plastic are safely cocooned in romantic communion, and co-senior waves 'thank you' as P-plater glances, drop-jawed through the window from her elevated SUV to see a mountainous protuberance aloft in the seat.

So that was co-senior's first problem.

The situation needed to be rectified with accelerated haste.

Parts died and fell off if they turned blue, and though a looky-looky wasn't possible, co-senior could have been an authentic group member in the Blue Man Group, singing to a different tune.

With a swift turnaround and frantic dash to the nearest shopping centre, co- senior slid out of the car with a gallant attempt at orienteering through back passages to avoid the boring of eyeballs from onlookers as their eyes travelled down past their mobile screens to the donkey rig thumping past their field of vision.

Co-senior, sweating profusely at the thought of amputation, couldn't be too close to people. Although there was no camouflage apparel available, he heroically and invincibly puffed up his self-esteem as he walked through same shopping centre, heading for the nearest washrooms.

At last, after wriggling through the food court, he arrived, only to find that this was the female door, and the male door was right on the opposite side of the centre.

In desperation, he ran to the opposite side, nuts knocking in a very accurate reproduction of Newton's cradle, and slammed open the door for serious relief.

And there, in front of him, was a miniature toddler toilet.

At this stage, at the risk of decapitation, this miniature piece of porcelain was the most welcome sight of the day. Bending low and eternally grateful for the bicep training, co-senior yanked with force and plastic bottle flew under the door to shin- kick little cherub waiting to practice his no-nappy toilet training. He was howling, his carer was nauseated, and one important appendage had had a very trying day.

Needless to say, there was no date night. The only date was prostrate on the bed making communion this time with an anti-inflammatory heating pad.

And then he suddenly woke up to find that the heating pad he had borrowed for his sore knee had drifted north, and his nighttime water bottle had emigrated from next to his bed to peek cheekily 'round the corner of the bathroom door.

FRIENDS

I WAS BORN.

I was the 'what happened' child.

I had brothers and sisters much older than me.

They were my first friends.

I had to be the best at everything to be noticed.

My nickname was 'Mrs Me-Too'.

I went to boarding school.

I married young.

I had children young.

I divorced young.

Lost most of my friends in the 'don't want to be disloyal phase'.

I married again.

I had more children.

I emigrated.

Lost friends who thought our new country was on another planet.

(Didn't have mobile phones or computers in those days, letter writing was tardy.)

Made new friends at the school gate.

Lost friends when children moved on.

Joined Amway.

Made LOTS of friends.

Stopped Amway.

Lost all of 'LOTS of friends'.

Started business.

Made friends.

Stopped business.

Not paying them anymore, so lost friends.

Made friends with children's friends.

They married and babied and moved countries.

Lost friends.

Semi-retired.

Made new friends.

See it happens to all of us…

BUT

There is a silver thread through every season.

It is the beautiful friends that hang around — those constant, real, there friends. Not the Facebook, Instagram, or electronic friends. Not the friends whose bodies and souls have been edited. These are the loneliest friends.

No, it's the 'I'm coming 'round right now in my PJs, crying on your shoulder, and eating an almond croissant' friends.

These are the friends I am talking about. These are the friends who make you laugh so hard your pelvic floor collapses. These are the friends who create the indelible memories. These are the friends who bring a glow, and when they leave, make you feel fuzzy.

For one of my significant birthdays, Croatia was the goal. All my children and any friends who could get there was my goal.

My beautiful friend and her hubby always get there, by hook or by crook. I love them as they remained in the camp many years ago when the environment got messy. They never judged. They never took sides. They are booming earlier than us, and international travel, although challenging, works well if they adhere partly to their routines and rituals.

My friend is quite gorgeous, likes to look gorgeous, is not averse to a little cosmetic help when needed, and is loyal to the core.

The day was glorious, sailing through little coves and jumping into the sea and the issue was resolved between the girls as to where we should dine (daughter-in-law leaned toward gourmet dining, daughter leaned toward atmosphere and vista). The consensus was to travel to an isolated island (atmosphere and vista) and dine on delicious Croatian delicacies (gourmet dining)—problem solved.

Well, not the whole problem!

The boat that ferried us was a high-speed rubber dinghy, and the only way on and off was kicking off our Jimmy Choos (only worn on very special birthday occasions) and trampolining in.

More of a problem was getting out.

Our strong 'uns grabbed our hands, sliding us onto the quay, leaving most of our feathered accessories permanently entwined in harmony with the wooden pier.

The return journey was more ominous.

It was a black night, no lights, and inexperienced boat captain. We didn't really worry as Bollinger had worked its magic. Until a shout from our concerned son pierced the silence: 'Stand up, we are about to hit a rogue!'

We all rose in unison, including a very pregnant daughter and several unbalanced senior citizens. We hung on tight, braced for action, and with that my friend's glorious, beautiful, coiffed, elegant wig flew off into the abyss, and we cried together with laughter as we greeted 'enchante' to her awry exposed wig cap.

Nothing mattered in that moment, same as nothing mattered when we bombed into the water the following day. My friend had gravitated to the mop as an ingenue new hairstyle, and my cellulite made perfect peace with the azure and welcoming sea. Nobody noticed, and nobody cared. It was friendship, raw and real.

Co-senior and I decided to start a business with a friend. This always takes trust supreme, innovation, imagination, and decisive branding. It was in the edible space.

Of course, a business needs a name. We flung around many ideas. They all had something, but just not that 'it' — the 'what the hell would you name the business that for, but I will never forget your business name "it".'

Eventually, we got it, we were certain that this was the perfect name.

Co-senior, who was our stabling influence, was uncertain, and in his usual due-diligent, manner checked it out. I might say he was rather smug in his grandiose reveal that it was, in fact, an anything-goes porn site. We collapsed in heartwarming giggles while imagining clients arriving at our premises ready for hanky-panky, only to find their sweet edibles were of a different kind.

When you get divorced and remarry, you bond with the new hubbie's besties. They either can't stand you and play hopscotch between the first Queen of the Castle and yourself, or they cut ties with the bygone and embrace with open arms.

It is daunting.

One can be over-the-top-lovely lovely or just be your own damn self.

Co-senior was showing off to his best mate. And while dutifully watching a 'death stare if you dare win in front of my new girlfriend' tennis match, I thought I rather liked this guy. He is interesting and artsy and unusual and outspoken.

Circling in after the match, while downing ales (one of the boys — aren't you proud of me?) best mate started throwing verbal curveballs, rather like his tennis game. I picked up my shoe, huge cloggy, in-fashion shoe, and threw it right at him. Bullseye! And we were friends and have been for forty-five years.

Friends are intergenerational, interdenominational, interracial, LGBTQ. If they get you, they just get you. They are at the heart of your heart and in completion make you whole.

Lunch with Girlfriends
By Kathy O'Malley

Elaine's vertigo has never been worse
Kay can't recall where she left her purse
Rhonda's about to replace her knees
Linda's breathing is tinged with a wheeze
Donna's left boob has a troublesome lump
Diane's on her third trip to take a dump
Lorraine's husband can't remember a thing
Nine years a widow, Marge still wears her ring
Marlene is dealing with another UTI
Sally's giving a hearing aid another try
Marie has decided she can't drive at night
Sharon still wears clothes two sizes too tight.
They've been through divorces and babies and wakes
They do for each other whatever it takes
They've already buried Marcia and Kate
And truthfully, Lizzie's not looking so great
So whenever they can, they get out to eat
Open bottles of wine and forget their sore feet.
There's laughing and crying and letting down guards
And when the bill comes, there's ten credit cards.
So here's to the waiters who keep orders straight
And to the places that let lunches run three hours late
And here's to the girlfriends, those near and far
Here's to the girlfriends, you know who you are.[1]

---

1   Kathy O'Malley, "Lunch with Girlfriends," Facebook, July 26, 2017, https://www.facebook.com/kathyandjudy/posts/recently-ate-at-a-restaurant-where-a-table-of-girlfriends-of-a-certain-age-were-/2066740723547132.

ORGASMIC OLDIES

WHO SAID THAT WE ARE DONE AND DUSTED? FOR goodness' sake—didn't Sarah procreate over ninety? Well, *that* chapter did actually make me dig deep. The mental imagery was just a bit disturbing.

Sexual subject matter and conversation doesn't dominate barbeque jamborees these days, though there may be a bit of nudge, nudge wink, wink here and there.

Prepping is the problem these days. Not the *MasterChef* kind of prepping, not al dente and chop chop—more slip slap slop kind of prepping.

Now in 'them' old days, prepping was fast and furious. In fact, everything was fast and furious. It's a different story now. Now we are simply persnickety.

Do you want to know what that word means?

It means all kinds of things such as innuendos, suggestion, breath in ear, post porn, 'I'll do it on my time' picky. We don't mean to be like that, but there is so much prep required these days to even consider any leg over, and there are so many steps to this process, which we can't always remember.

So, the physical is probably challenge number one. Who wants to play footsy when the temperature is subzero? There is nothing sexy about that. We seniors are 'enoughly' shrivelled. Our interior volume has shrunk, thank God, but our sub-elastic covering can't keep up, and hence, our corrugated body artwork.

We know our co-seniors love to cling on to this residual, but hey, we will always be trained to suck it up. Oops, did I say that!

And why the hell the aftershave and the quick shower? It takes five seconds, yes, five seconds to abort take off, so we just don't have wiggle room. No aftershave, please, especially on the trombone. The taste of fragrance is only for the big departmentals. Oh, I can see how you did misconstrue—you are on point with the big departmentals. But, a little nudge here, these are our olfactories, and we want primal, musty, earthy. We don't want to bang Eau Sauvage.

Music on, music off, what genre on?

Is it easy-listening, romantic love songs, breathe-in, breathe-out music?

Do we want memories of our last spa visit? Maybe that is a good thing, as it keeps the blood pressure down when we really want it to go up.

Should we lock into the Top 50, rapping Eminem?

Maybe the '60s will do it for us, but maybe it dates us. I know, Barry Manilow; that will make us winners all round.

Now, we need to talk about accoutrements. I saw some inventive toys advertised on the back page of some magazine I was reading at the hairdresser. There were definitely some unusual contraptions. Some of these innovative newbies were hard to understand. Where the hell would you put them?

And everything seems to vibrate. Who designs these?

Do we really need our bits to buzz?

And that monstrous purple contraption! Who does purple? It seems rather kinky but doesn't float my boat.

And we better advise the manufacturers that monstrous doesn't work these days. Everything is dry, and we don't want another hernia to puncture our abdomen.

Maybe this is a little too close for comfort for some seniors in denial, or should I say, denial in seniors. But, despite the practicalities, there can be hilarious as well. Lift off is not always a certainty, and a little trip to the 'extended family, who knows everything about you, GP' produces a little, blue Pfizer accessory that jiggles in co-senior's pocket while drinking wine and downing spaghetti bolognaise in an extremely romantic pre-prep ceremony.

Co-senior and I know each other, I mean, really know each other, so when I saw ardent fixated eyes, my first thought was maybe there had been an explosion of floaters. Spag bol nearly landed fair and square in my lap of luxury. Table, husband, plates, knives, spoons, glasses, wine, water, salt, and pepper rose triumphantly preparing for a volcanic eruption. Beware, Boomers, medicated encouragement should remain in home privacy.

A perpendicular penis should not be guiding you home. We have Google Maps now, for goodness' sake!

Orgasmic we still are, us Boomers—could be for custard or chocolate or Netflix.

But don't underestimate the twinkle, we still got it, albeit a touch scarcer and a touch slower. It may gross you out, but hey, there is still *Something about Mary*.

THE SUPERMARKET BUFFET

PEOPLE ARE SO MEAN.

Is it because we walk slower, look greyer, or are simply an object of rebuke for our years of hard work and overindulgence in our gifts, time, and heart?

I don't know, but what I do know is that it is getting worse.

Take, for instance, my little outing today.

It wasn't too daunting, wasn't meant to take time, and my practice of smiling (or maybe call it grinning) at everyone should surely have ensured a skip through the daisies for all the passing recipients.

It augured to be a good quick trip, in and out, with a coffee and eco bags that, thank goodness, I had at last remembered to bring with me. Everything was neatly balanced in the trolley and home, James.

Nah, wasn't going to be that easy.

My plan was to make fresh strawberry souffle for guests tomorrow, but now needles had been found hidden in the juicy innards—some tampering from a disgruntled employee, they say.

I mean, from what I understand, in medieval Christian art this beautiful luscious, aromatic, juicy morsel symbolizes spiritual purity, decency, and righteousness. Come on, disgruntled employee, go learn your history!

So, no strawberry mousse. Pity, as it is one of my pièce de résistance dishes, the 'recipe you don't give out to friends' dish.

And to make it worse, the guests are true gourmands, and I could easily stuff up my second option.

Banana flambé could work, but in my earnest forage for the just-ripe ingredient, I missed the skin on the floor (could have been my multifocals, actually), lazily discarded by a 'get a piece of fruit free' child, slipped, stumbled, didn't land on the glossy floor but ignominiously headfirst in the sizeable display of avocados.

Even up to this point, I am still positive. I brush off mangled skin and flesh, or should I say, *wiped* it off, remarking to all around that I am having a guacamole experience sans tomatoes. It's the new thing, actually.

So what has this got to do with the buffeted generation?

Well, it was the Gen Z, Gen Y, Gen X, or should we say, Gen Stress day today.

Everyone was rushing around, it seemed, with workloads off the Richter, waiting in line to retire the Boomers and grab the power.

Every tab is open, brain crash is imminent, and electronics now seem to be a vital body part.

These ones today look anxious, irritable, and angry. They are shitty trolley pushers, and they rolled over my foot without even a blink of apology, and it was damned sore.

And, to make it worse, it was the first day of spring. My new yellow sandals had had their first outing, and now they had the Great Wall of China embedded in their colour scheme.

So, then the inevitability of checkout, and I could feel the invisible force behind me, impatiently stomping and sighing. A little adjustment forward seemed necessary to avoid ankle fracture.

And then, Mr Pink-shirted, Goiter-eye, iPhone-glued-to-ear Shopper had a hot-tempered verbal eruption, spewing forceful verbal bile, accusing hip attachment, bill payment suggestion and a new entry in the revised dictionary — unless I didn't really understand some of the expletives.

This was buffeting — the real unadulterated, abusive, keep-your-hat-on buffeting.

But don't buffet this senior. You see, I am a cruiser. I know all about huge wave buffeting, and I'm damn ready for the pomposity and downright disrespect.

After a hefty comeback — I was actually quite proud of *my* command of abusive language adjectives — he winced, squirmed, and shrunk visibly, sort of like those big, brave, loud, angry dogs who retreat when the passing Chihuahua gives them a mouthful. On reconsidering, I wasn't really proud of myself but at best I stood my ground.

But, hooray, I had now encountered buffet two and survived, and all I was trying to accomplish was a supermarket run. Passing word of advice here — look them straight in the eyes while you do your buffeting. It's seriously much more effective.

There was only one last movement to the car, and supermarket buffets are done for the day, but as you surely know, it's an 'everything happens in three' phenomena, so brace for completion.

My car is little, but you know I love it.

The newborns, however, in the carparks are another story.

I can't see if there is even a driver in the seat from behind my steering wheel vantage. And I can't open my door, as they have claimed the yellow dividing line. This means a passenger-door entry and a long jump over the gear stick.

Thank goodness my numbers were down in the weight loss meeting this week, or it would have been a cerebral anxious return to the Thai cave-rescue emotion.

Now, some decision had been made in the centre that motor vehicles needed to Pacman out of there in some unusual combinations. I know when it's dual lane or single lane or only-go-right lane. I am happily ready to go home, coffee in hand, picking at a polenta cake and 'crumbing' violently.

A huge SUV bounds around the corner, and I am barricaded. Now we have an impasse. Sorry to say another Gen Stress. I can't reverse — a long lineup of cars is behind. Can't go forward — goalkeeper SUV is straddled across the exit. So it's pretty much a sticky situation.

With that, Gen Stress rolls down the window and condescendingly advises that we are in a two-way situation, which of course, I know. I was born in this carpark, for God's sake.

She stands her ground, forcing the whole line of vehicles to retreat for madame to glide her leviathan into its preferred abode. Forgot to mention that this was with a raised second finger and a 'f*#% off, old woman' thrown in.

Thank God, I had my polenta cake. It calmed things down, but it was ready and able for combat, and any further abuse could have landed a cake plant in the face. Well, maybe that was not such a good idea. After all, old-timer experience should really set a better example.

The morning was unpleasant, but a big thanks to the long-haired tradie in the queue at checkout who rolled his eyes and rolled up his sleeves and turned to me to say: 'You'll be fine. I got this, I got this', as he puffed up to take on Mr Pink Shirt. I was relieved to see that there are still angels out there, even if I hadn't noticed.

If you sometimes adjust your glasses, you will be able to see them more clearly.

THE SEPARATE-BEDROOM SYNDROME

CO-SENIOR SNORES, A RUMBLING, LOUD-FREIGHT-TRAIN, window-rattling snore. And now he tells me that I also snore and is well invested in researching all Ted Talks on sleep apnea and conditions that cause, fix, and laugh about this condition.

I was walking around in a haze so bad that it took time to work out how to brush my teeth.

With it came the grumpy 'angry bird' who hadn't had enough sleep and wasn't coping.

Where has happy, positive Julie gone, people would say? Do you want to know? I am engulfed in the noises of a train journey across Mongolia, and I can't get off.

So, then, the discussion ensued about sleeping in different rooms. Not moving out, just sleeping, so we could get back to normal function. It felt a bit weird and friend-zone like, and we both didn't like it. Where were the snuggle-sock cuddles and late-night analysis of the world's problems? Where was holding each other's hands—avoiding the arthritic knuckle—till we dropped off peacefully for the first tiny little moment?

Lack of sleep won over, and it was time.

Co-senior and I reluctantly made up the bed next door. Lucky that it was co-senior who was ejecting and not me. I could remain in my cosy little environment and even scroll through Instagram and Facebook before beddy-byes without reprimand about blue light-reducing melatonin.

Then, co-senior started getting used to it. He liked reading at night. I couldn't, as my multifocals could never find the sweet spot, and the anxiety of non-vision and the fear of glaucoma was a veritable sleep deterrent.

So, I retaliated by switching on the TV to watch some droning war documentary or a weekly crime show. But the guns and shots and blood loss were now firmly engrained in the brain before drop-off, causing vivid embellishment of the dream that ensued.

When together, I liked the air conditioner cool. Co-senior was under the air conditioner so was transported to Alaska and breathed in the little feather outputs that flew out of the filter, adding spluttering and coughing to the rumbling mix. This, while I was warmly snuggled in my perfect sleep condition, wishing vociferously to fall asleep quickly so as not to create ear damage.

Back to us in separate rooms.

Co-senior needed bathroom visits that were not in sync with mine, so we would pass each other in the night trying to feel our way to expulsion, only to knock over the water bottle next to the bed that flooded into our shoes and seeped into the bed linen.

Wakey-wakey during the night was par for the course. Sleeplessness attracted a quick switch on of the phone and a glance at whether any overseas callers had touched base while we were 'sleepy-time'.

Switch off was more precarious, as this often resulted in a neat deposit into the glass of water on the bedside table, which was ready and waiting for nighttime thirst.

It took a while, and the routine settled in. It felt strange but made us more in love with each other during the day as we energized together and took on life full tilt.

We didn't talk about it, as it felt 'unmarried', until there were little slips here and there from friends.

One had a wonky hip, another a wonky prostrate.

One needed magnesium, and another a splint.

One stole the pillows, others the doona.

One farted loud, and the other burped in tandem.

Sleep for all was a veritable mess.

We don't talk about this, and we don't share this in the friendship circles, but now we are becoming so much more honest with each other. Most are cohabitating this way and love each other no less. We can spread out and take over some of the other's wardrobe.

We can read late into the night, burp and fart with enjoyment, and love the quiet morning cuddles by the one who happens to wake up first.

I did just that this morning. I realized, however, that I need to be on it more often. In my bedroom absence, the status quo has changed.

Co-senior leaned over and stroked my face. I was expecting gentle as usual, but it was not to be.

Co-senior had been surfing the late-night shopping channel, and he was now the very proud owner and wearer of two rough, creviced, anti-arthritic Michael Jackson gloves.

QUIET IS NOT DAUNTING, IT'S PRECIOUS

IT'S QUIET IN OUR HOUSE TODAY. SO STILL.

There are no neighbour's cars revving up for quick exit. There are no kookaburras chanting their morning melodies. There are no airbusses overhead transporting loved ones over the ocean to touch the hearts of their offspring who have spread their wings to live in other lands.

There is just silence, and it is beautiful.

We are all living these days in this jangled cacophony of disruption, multi-tasking with myriad of choices.

Technology has taken over our homes, and we are prisoners to beeps and pings and tones and tunes. For us seniors, this is a completely new world. We leave our homes daily to join the wave of ADD, and our nervous systems are getting rattled.

We are all never off; we are contactable everywhere. We are our life's computer server waiting to serve the known and the unknown with rapid return of communication, and if we don't, we are barraged once again in some other form. It's all so noisy.

Everyone is anxious trying to tick off their to-do lists, which they never complete. Parents are present but not 'present', which is eventually mimicked by their children, who display the same freneticism in their day-to-day routine.

I say STOP.

It doesn't have to be like this.

This can be done better, but only if we have the discipline to switch off this life noise and intrusion. Take control of the noise while you still can hear.

This is not a 'when we', but I recall walking with bare feet to the local deli to buy a vanilla ice cream cone and feed the remnants of the cone to ducks swimming in a pond nearby. The awareness of each step in the sand was the only sound, with the occasional 'duck quack' intruding and everywhere else just silence.

I remember clambering over the neighbour's fence to kick a ball and laugh as we collected flowers from the garden for our mum. The only sound was our laughter and an occasional bee foraging for nectar. Now we don't even know our neighbours, or if we do, it's to complain about their noisy boomboxes spitting out rap.

There are layers of noise everywhere, and we need to dissect them and switch off the unimportant.

Day-to-day life is noisy.

Highways are noisy.

Colleagues are noisy.

Technology is noisy.

Modems are noisy.

Grandchildren are noisy.

IT'S ALL NOISY!!!!

But if we peel back the layers, we will find we can concentrate again on the single all-encompassing sounds of a wave breaking, the wind rustling, a baby gurgling, a bird calling, and it's peaceful, uncomplicated, raw, and completely mindful in its simplicity.

Co-senior and I have plans to move sometime in the future from our little bubble of silence to less maintenance and less expense. We sometimes believe that the future may be swathed in silence so strong that its eventual osmosis is into boredom. We pray that we make the right decision and don't get stuck between foreign cabbage-cooking odours and bawdy late-night brawls that pierce the luxury that we have been able to enjoy in the presence of today.

Maybe the silence is in our mind. We have created this mindfulness, and we take it with us wherever we go. It is not boredom. It is not emptiness. It is present, it is now, and it is so gloriously peaceful that it is so very, very precious.

CRUISE SOLUTION

—

I HAD A GOOD HEART-TO-HEART WITH MY CHILDREN THIS week.

Their beef was that we were not like Mr and Mrs So-and-So, who looked after their grandchildren from dawn to dusk every day—and skipped through the process merrily.

I gently informed my offspring that co-senior and I were getting older, and made other little insidious excuses to confirm that at this stage in our lives, this was not our life mission.

We were married with children and had children tied to our ankles right from the beginning. I might add that we were both left, and so brought our little bundles of joy with us to our second union.

Our offspring were aghast! Weren't we meant to love their own offspring, never want them out of our sight, and be the first thought when we opened our eyes? Well, yes, we do adore them, but after much admonishment and guilt buildup, it was now time to set things straight.

There are grandparents who have nothing to do with their grandchildren. Such a loss, I agree, as the little nippers are really quite gorgeous in their innocence and add dimension to our aging status.

There are grandparents who look after their grandchildren day in and day out and day in and day out. Don't know how they do it, really. But as I mentioned to aggrieved parents, these nannas and pappas probably have homes emptier than a crypt. They then endlessly play hide-and-seek and watch *Paw Patrol*, begging for some laughter, noise, and messiness created by their little chaos machines. I say this category of 'golden-agers' are sadly lonely, or bored, or are getting paid for their attention to the clan while their own offspring fly off to work to pay the daily bills and take a breath in adult company.

And then there is the 'us'.

That's the category we fall into.

We adore our 'littlies'; we are superman/woman in emergencies. We are present, yes, really present when it's our time, and we don't present with any 'damn'.

We relish in rolling around on the floor as 'Mrs Boob Tube' or drawing unicorns and rainbows on bank deposit receipts.

We adore being elevated to 'Gagga, you're the best, best cooker' as chocolate icing finds its way into every nook and cranny of the kitchen with each sensory movement of licking the spoon. It's all-in, and it's explosive joy simply in the knowledge of knowing that it is only for a while, and then it's jettison time back to mummy or daddy or carer.

The chaos and return is blissful.

I asked a friend who was about to retire what his plans were for the next couple of months. His reply was that he had booked three long cruises back to back. I get it; we love cruises as well. But three cruises back to back? It seemed like an endless lymphatic drainage treatment.

He had six granddaughters, and he was tired of dressing up in tutus and being poked and tattooed by permanent lipsticks. He may as well have been an Uber driver for the school lifts that he had done and had lost the energy in dealing with being equitable with his three daughters-in-law, who tallied the score as to equal-committed involvement with each and every one of the offspring.

It didn't matter where he was, on the massage table, playing golf, in the pub with friends, or just enjoying some solace scrolling LinkedIn on the toilet. He would be found.

I mean, he could have just ignored 'By the Seaside', the allocated ringtone for 'babysit time'. But the addiction of guilt should there be an emergency was so gut-blowing that he was compelled to press the little green phone and connect.

There was no escape, no hiding place for quiet reverie.

And then along came the cruise solution.

Wi-Fi was far too expensive for continuous chats, remoteness was tracked on cruise tracker and dance groups, open-air movies and brain-numbing cocktails were substantially included in the over-the-sea adventure.

No grubby fingers to wash, no dinosaur books to read, no butts to wipe clean, and no interruptions while reading the adventures of Christian Grey.

Glancing along the line of chaise longues positioned at the pool, it seemed that we were not alone in our escapology but were joined by a whole nation of nannas and pappas doing exactly the same.

Sorry, my precious offspring, you are my life, you know that, and your offspring are my soul, and I do really miss all my glorious little bundles of grubbiness. But there is a time for everything, and now is our time, and just for this moment we just gotta say, 'Sea Ya Later'.

IT'S OK TO BE MISERABLE NOW AND THEN

IT ALL STARTED THIS MORNING WITH THE DAMN SCALE.

My trusted measurement machine centres my day—little bit up, little bit down. That's OK, but when it's 'oh my goodness, how did this happen' up, then the day doesn't start too well.

Now I have to be honest, it was co-senior's scale. My scale only reveals half the picture. Shower wetness has seeped into the display, the zero looks like an *8* or a backward *C*, and now I have no mood barometer.

So I try co-senior's scale, and just for back up, another scale firmly hidden behind the sheets in the linen cupboard, and for back up back up, the flimsy light contraption I find in my last suitcase from a 'keep it real' cruise.

But, nah, even though the numbers between scales were very independent in their readings, I was goddamn up! And the worst part—the chocolate brownie of which I did not imbibe was still sitting on the kitchen counter, and I couldn't barrel down fast enough to stuff my mandibles to make me feel better, or not!

To reassure body-image pundits who spruik gushingly about love the 'who you are', this isn't about weight (or maybe just a

smidgeon about weight). Letterbox is full of glossy spring entice-
ments, full of spring floral fashion, and I want 'em.

But realistically, this daily three o'clock denial of the cake,
brownie, torte is about making sure that the numbers are pretty on
the blood pressure monitor, making sure that the life pump keeps
on pumping.

So then my neck hurts.

This makes the outer edges of my cerebellum very murky.

OK, so I've been through the scenario of 'I have a brain
tumour', or MS or never-ending neuralgia or mercury poisoning
and 'I don't ever get a headache, so has my phone finally built a
new antennae close to my temporal lobe'.

Stressed it all.

Then, admonishing myself, I remember it's very simple. The
culprit is the four- hour conversation with my new friend I met on
the weekend at a seventieth bash. She embraced my left-hand side,
resulting in a rigid four-hour, upper body twist. Thinking positively, this could become a new yoga position. And this left manoeuvre
had been very necessary to avoid the ho hum of prostrates and
short-seller conversations that were going on, on my right.

But another little thought wafted through. Maybe it could be
dehydration.

I read an article that said I am meant to drink Lake Louise
in volume every day. That's all well and good, but we are Boomers, and we have to make damn sure that the dam wall is closed
and evacuation doesn't happen too fast. We all have pelvic floor
dropsy in some shape or form, or so the ads say when spruiking
their wares.

So now that every hypochondriacal condition has looped, I
am on to all the catastrophes in the world. Today the news report-
ed that there was a sickening assault, trapped miners, serial killer
manhunt, measles outbreak, Meghan Markle outfit fail—good
news day all in all, but it is messing with my brain.

War has been declared in my brain between mind-numbing sensationalism and mind-numbing affirmations, and today, I don't know which side will be victorious. Coz today I am miserable.

So then the phone bill. Did we phone Mars this month? The amount is so monstrous that I have to play hopscotch between accounts to ensure continued service.

We are early adaptors, but an electric vehicle is not yet ensconced in the garage, plugged in consistently, and our air conditioner isn't even working.

And then we explain the whole situation to Jasmina in the Philippines, who says she completely understands but can't do much about it. The explanation of Boomer hardship does nothing to the outcome, and I can almost sense an under-the-breath mutter of 'just pay your bloody bill!'

It's nine degrees outside, and nothing is warm. I can't find the hot water bottle, so I sit miserably in front of the television listening to the parliamentary argy-bargy trying to work out how to keep us all warm without mortgaging our lifespan.

And the f@!!%#!!! bush turkeys!

They are enough to make us scream in frustration. We have erected wire, tiles, bushes, anything we can find. Nothing, absolutely nothing, stops the incessant, entitled mound building.

The garden looks like a tsunami's aftermath, and it's all because the newly arrived neighbours have decided they are such pretty birds and feed them high tea with various birdy delicacies.

Stock market is declining.

Superannuation is declining.

House prices are declining.

Height is declining.

Lifespan is declining.

No wonder I am miserable.

I go to the supermarket to get lost in the chocolate aisle. And then some doddery senior following his co-senior's list, ambling on the wrong side of the aisle, blocks the flow and rolls his specials-laden trolley over my foot!

The family is being nasty, the kids' therapists put all the blame for everything in their lives on me, and the dog just 'shat' on my new Temple and Webster carpet.

Now I am really miserable.

Oh my goodness, this is so horrible in its self-indulgence in the face of real misery and hardship.

I do know and care about global hunger.

I do know and care about poverty in third-world countries.

I do know and care about the homeless in America and the underprivileged in Australia.

I do know and care about it all.

I know, I know, I know.

I also know that I am being selfish and moody and entitled and ungracious.

But it is only today.

I am, in fact, lucky, fortunate, loved, blessed, and forgiven.

Thank goodness, I am downright miserable today, because it will make tomorrow so much more relevant and sweet.

STUFF CRIPPLES

ARE YOU DROWNING IN STUFF, FELLOW SENIORS? IS YOUR day spent cleaning up each room and putting things back into their place—if you can remember what that place is? When did you last touch the book smothered in mould on the bottom shelf of the tool cupboard in the garage?

Why are we keeping all this stuff? It's stuffing with our brains.

I know, I know, we 'may need it someday' or we 'are going to read it someday'. I know we are keeping it because we remember the experience when we bought it or the smell of Mum lingers on her decaying handbag in the archive box.

Let's face it— really face it—what the hell can we take with us when we go? It is all just loaned to us. Things don't really matter. If we haven't used it, it is not useful; we don't love it, and there is no emotional attachment. Ditch!!

It's hard, isn't it? It's the circle of life thing. We spend all this time searching out the *perfect*. The perfect furniture and accessory and outfit and stuff. And then our taste changes in different seasons, but we can't bear to ditch the goodies from the fading season. Why?

So, are we really happy engulfed by things?

It reminds me of those balls at Ikea. They are fun for a while, then you are sinking right inside them all. You peek your head up above the colours just to snatch a breath.

That's the same with stuff.

So now it's time, Boomers, to learn about all the 'ditch' companies out there. Some can actually bring in a pretty penny.

First and foremost is eBay.

Everything seems to tick along smoothly until some random person decides not to collect or pay and then puts up some shady report about how you never posted off. Give it right back to them, seniors. They may think they are fancy pants giving you a bad review, but if you give it right back, it is not going to look too fine and dandy for them, now is it?

Then there's Gumtree.

It's fun scrolling through page after page of goodies that need to find a new lover.

It's all varied, some functional, some a bargain, and some plain weird, like 'Bottled Air from a Justin Bieber concert' to a British army tank cherished by some fervent collector.

But what a thrill when the kist you haven't opened since the '60s finds a happy new home and the techno-gadgie you advertised, as per the outer wrapping, but never used and don't really know what to use it for, rakes in a healthy dollar and dark exchange in front of a McDonald's drive-through.

Ahh, the thrill of the hobbyist entrepreneur.

The cash-filled envelope starts to 'tizzle' the imagination. Shut it down, Boomers—don't spend it on more stuff. Use it to cruise to the Galapagos or senior rock-chick guitar lessons.

Now that would shake up the grand chillies.

Of course, if nobody wants your beautiful century-old writing desk from generations past, and you've tried every avenue from antique store, individual, advertisements, or garage sale, then plonk it loudly on Ziilch and suddenly some expert will find it delightful and hire a truck to take it away to its new home. The century-old leg may fall off, but they got it for nothing, so refunds are not in the plan.

And of course, there is the tried-and-tested garage sale.

Make pretty signs in bold writing. Hang these signs on neighbourhood trees, and don't freak on the next drive past after a heavy thunderstorm to find that the poster is now 'tears of a clown.' Just remember to take them down, though, if it doesn't make your local council happy.

Expect to make thousands; it will keep you buoyant. But, darling seniors, it will most likely be hundreds. Brew a big pot of tea to sip in quiet moments, have eyes in the back of your head for nimble fingers, and make sure the door into the house is firmly locked to ensure that your latest guitar doesn't become part of the spoils.

Take turns with co-senior, if there is one, but brief co-senior very well to make sure he doesn't put his own slant on the price and you watch your Christofle frame thrown in as a bonus for the spider catcher.

And, if all else fails, enjoy the incessant chats with people who have nowhere else to go on a sunny Saturday morning.

So, dear Boomers, tear down the museum and make room for the present. Know what you really, really need and what brings you joy. Have no guilt.

Physical space and mental space go hand in hand. The disarray of too much stuff clutters our brain and we all need air and light to grow. Memories remain even if they are not solid and in front of you.

Let go, however painful it may feel at just that moment. Your stuff is holding you back. Don't you want to dream and do and own nothing that has a hold on you?

Throw them away; you won't believe how cathartic the whole process can and will be.

I'M MAGNIFICENTLY MAGNIFICENT

—

Today I was magnificently magnificent.

My sixty-five-year-old body bounded out of bed thinking it was twenty-five.

Make up — perfect.

Hair — glorious.

Outfit — Sarah Jessica Parker chic with LV bag swung over my shoulder and an attitude to fit. I strode out of the house with my head held high and my self-esteem even higher.

I was perfectly intact.

The morning involved various meetings in various situations with various groups. I was confident and brought much more than experience and insight to the table.

Noooo, I brought the whole damn degustation to the table.

I was on a roll; I was Superwoman.

After a long day and feeling splendidly relevant, I arrived back home ready for a cuppa. I threw my over-priced accessory onto the bed, and in a sideward glance, I caught my silhouette slurking across the mirror. I froze and cautiously turned.

Standing in front of me was the woman who had started the morning with a powerful 'tude.

There she was, in gay abandon, in glorious reveal.

There she was in her tunic top, and panning down, there she was gloriously exposed in her fully opaque, constricting, magnificent see-through leggings.

Oh yes, I had thought I was pulling on my trousers that morning. I didn't know and wasn't aware.

But what I did know is that it all begins and ends in the mind.

What you give power to has power over you if you allow it.

And that day I didn't allow it—I was simply magnificently magnificent.

*

Knitting has become my new hobby.

A TED Talk this morning was effusing about the love of knitting, and I thought at last I was in very good, salubrious company.

I could just be vacant while my little fingers ran a marathon.

It kept me away from the peanut butter sandwich and spoonfuls of milo, and I could multitask watching my mindless reality.

The problem, therein, is that I am not crafty. You know, the crafty where a beautiful outfit is whipped up in one inhale, where a designer cake is designed in a whisk, where ceramics fly flawlessly from the oven. Knitting is a creative feat.

My take is that it is artistic and unique, and I can choose exactly the hue that works for me.

I wore my jumper today with glorious satisfaction (only in home security, I might add).

I was close to becoming famous as the extinct woolly mammoth favourite relative.

Few little problems, though.

I had knitted a plain row when it should have been purl. Only realizing halfway through the row that this was evolving, I was clueless as to how to reverse down the highway of the knitting needle.

So, it's now called *design*. How unique is that?

For sure, no one else has my pattern as I am (tongue in cheek) an innovator, a creator, an abstract-pattern maker.

It progressed from there, and spiralled down at rapid pace.

There were more dropped stitches, increases replaced decreases, and the result? A pothole bunchy design with unusual add-ons and a rather innovative perimeter, I may add.

I boldly walked into the knitting shop.

Everyone appeared rather snooty in their knitting aptitude and accomplishments while they rabbited on about their herringbone stitch and diagonal basket weave fit for a Markle Sparkle.

With a needle resembling an Amazonian centipede, I ventured toward finishing off my current hobby.

At last, it was completed.

I slipped it over my head in expectant apprehension.

Well, I can now see why I needed to be feeling this way.

Yes, the front and back did have unusual design elements. There were also some well-explored caves dotted around with protrusions of rainbow elements.

I had had to reverse the reverse of the reverse to sew the sleeves into the main body of the garment and formulate into the gaping armpits. I arranged it with perfect attention and perfect precision.

And then, reveal.

One sleeve perfectly in place—I did it!

Second sleeve glared at me with dominant intrusion. It was sewn inside out, and a convoluted thick scar of seam travelled down the whole length of my arm.

There was now no way back.

I wear this jumper with pride (only at home, mind you).

It proved to me that anything is worth a try, and I am starting again in fuchsia pink. It may be hideously unusual to you but to me, it is magnificently magnificent.

*

So, daughter-in-law asked me to babysit.

I adore, adore, adore, adore my grandbaby.

Did I say I adore my grandbaby?

He is a year and a half, and his sunshine smile is so brilliant that it soars through my soul.

When he sees his Gagga and Pappa, he is the cartwheel king and flings himself unceremoniously into the air for a smother of 'cuggles'.

Babysitting is as regular as we are able, as the tyranny of distance and the icy cold in winter prevents a weekly occurrence.

'Hi, Mum, 'bye, Mum' is pretty standard from all children, by the way. They can't wait to commute as adults without the 'convo' of textures and colours of evacuation.

We have very specific instructions.

Steam oven works like this, lasagne eaten with this, meatballs in case lasagne doesn't work.

Not going to go the banana route—had one choke on that already, and we know that conical and babies don't co-exist well.

Bath time is at this time, teeth before bath, toys in bath, cream after bath, music and stories before bed, bottle and cuddles in bed, lullabies, sleepy time music, pillow out, monitor on, sleeping bag snug, stars twinkling on the roof, and sign off.

Got it!!!

The kids close the door behind them, and they are out of there.

I hear them flying down the corridor with not a single backward glance.

As soon as the farewells are given, things don't exactly go as planned.

Stuff the lasagna… nah, meatballs… nah, fruit… nah, vegan bread… nah, hemp organic yoghurt… nah, Gagga and Pappa are in town—scramble for the rice bubble baby snacks and fruit squeezie puree and baby bell cheese and button yoghurts.

Yes, Gagga, that's the go—but don't tell.

OK, my precious…our secret. Not until you are twenty-one.

Bath time is splash time. Love the toothpaste as an after-dinner mint. More…

Woosh-cream is beautifully sliding down the wall, love AC/DC—what's this lully lully lullabies?

'Cuggles in bed with me, please, Gagga.'

'Don't like patting, hate the sleeping bag.'

And when the hell are Mamma and Dadda coming home?

'SCREAMMMMMM…'

Babysit fail!!!

He is alive—that's all that matters. We are his idols, and he thinks Pappa and Gagga are always and will always be his magnificently magnificent.

Social media is a thing—yeh!!! You've got to be with it to be with it.

Some people have millions of followers. That is supposed to be good. I have ten—I think. It seems to change depending on the whim and interest. That's pretty good, I reckon, as it's probably the only ten people in our demographic friend list that know how to work the damn thing.

I must say, though, that everybody's world, gym membership, children, achievements are so very perfect in their exquisiteness on these mediums. I mean, how the hell do you look so skinny when you work in the bakery, and my God, if I see another star diploma Kumon award, I'm going to gag. It all looks so perfectly wonderful.

So, time to participate, I presume.

I could start a LinkedIn account, but what the hell am I going to call myself? I could put down all my achievements from fifty years ago, but I don't do what I did then.

I haven't worked in an industry I was educated in. Don't really know why not; maybe life just took another turn.

It's going to be the big insta reveal.

So, it's time to scroll through photos and decide which ones work.

Should it be the authentic aspect or the downright ridiculously beautiful photoshopped moment? I'm pretty tempted.

No, I think I'll go authentic—maybe a little foray into this new, out-there 'cloud' world, with a little deposit of a good hair day, looking-good-drinking-champagne day, co-senior-handsome day.

I'm getting seduced very quickly.

Maybe it's the way to go, as some of my school friends may pick up and well, you know…

I go to 'photos', as I know I am supposed to do—haven't I been smart? I tick the photo that I want to reveal, do the sending and pushing and hashtag hashtag hashtag 'don't know why' process, and push.

Did it.

Holy shit—the photo of my divineness was right next to a photo of a bum flap that I had asked co-senior to take to see if maybe I was dying of some progressive disease. The tick had multiplied onto this print as well, and there in all its glory was my little mountain of floppability totally ex-po-sed to the world.

And I was absolutely clueless of how to edit and delete.

Yes, there I was, peoples of the world. There I was, bum in the air, magnificently exposed in its magnificently magnificent.

RADIO TO NETFLIX

OH, THE JOY!

Saturday night, lying in bed with the tiny transistor radio glued to the ear under the pillow, listening to the top twenty. What a treat it was, and even more joyful when our favourite cult hit screamed to number one and we knew that we had saved enough pocket money to race out and buy the — yes, let's say it — LP.

Ah, the radio, crackling its message through news and music and hot hits and drama — our connection to the world, and the creatives it had to offer. We fell in love with the tonal voices and imagined the beautiful faces behind the monologues that sometimes didn't match the teen cult mags where we buried our aspirations.

But time evolved, and evening home radio became unfashionable. The cathode-ray tube emerged, and we stayed glued to test patterns as the new form of entertainment launched into lounge rooms. We snuggled around little grey boxes, now seeing and hearing, and a new era was born.

The unfortunate radio had progressed further down the ladder as we could purchase audio reel-to-reel tapes — this the mark of a true audiophile and, for me, a little slice of heaven being able to record four different harmonies between tracks and channel my Joni Mitchell.

And vinyl records—don't know why they were called vinyl as they were made of a shellac substance—total addiction. Just picturing a cover of a favourite band and lyrics on the back, and we all became self-made superstars, spruiking karaoke in groups that helped us to find our beds after a long Saturday night.

Then movie night—the ultimate date night. A date synonymous with popcorn and fizzy cool drinks, far too large and far too expensive. Sometimes it was under the stars, at popular drive-ins where the post disgorged a large ugly speaker attached to the window and each one joggled for the best position to see past the steering wheel. No one needed to dress up, kids were snuggled between mountains of blankets and pillows, first dates were amorous and teenagers snuck in a few more than counted, hidden well below the mounds of bedding.

Today, movie night is still date night, but where are the people? Only a few heads rise above the seats, and they are usually peppered with grey. Even an opening screening of the latest offering has scattered attendance unless, of course, it is part of the Marvel cinematic brilliance. Movies are expensive and the nibbles even more, so who wouldn't bunker in at home and dial up one of the latest, all warm and fuzzy on the living room couch, armed with home-popped popcorn and a good bottle of red?

We seniors still love to indulge in a night amongst life and the big screen. We grab a cinemaphile friend, choose a genre, and settle in for a story telling night feeding our imagination. Sometimes, alas, we can fall into forgetful syndrome and work out that we have seen the movie already, but that's all right, as we still can't remember how the story ends. We sink down into the velvety seats and pray hard that our germophobic skulls don't collect a few head lice on the way.

Modern-day home dial ups are confusing, are they not? The channel changers are minimal, and the sliding flat surface to find what one is looking for is a whole procedure. Our fingers are chunkier with age (and it's not just our fingers), as we swish from left to right, never finding the sweet spot.

We land up in frantic frustration on *Rosemary's Baby* rather than Elmo, which we have now inadvertently purchased and has been charged to the children's account. Do we leave a sticky note on the TV to say that we have squandered their babysitting money? Maybe not; it's just payback for taping Donald Duck over our precious wedding video.

Netflix and *streaming* are now the buzzwords around dinner tables, and we are feeling quite hipster. We have no idea how to set it all up and rely on family visits. These are few and far between, as the 'burbs' seem past the long divide, and it usually ends up in a desperation call to an Airtasker to do the job.

Leads are untwisted and inserted, and before we know it, we are live, but heaven help us if anything freezes, as we are clueless as to how to put it all together again and we didn't even take notes.

These days, however, we challenge ourselves as we channel surf the nine hundred-plus channels, never finding quite the right place to halt. We zap between channels during commercial breaks, and then are so far down the content line that we forget where we were before and have to start all over again watching the end of something we are clueless how it started.

It takes so much time to even decide on where to park our eager brains.

The choice is so formidable, and the choice so huge that we longingly reverie back to the days of four channels and five o'clock game shows.

Eventually, we capitulate, although the night is still young. Our brains are befuddled and perplexed.

We switch off and head for the storage cupboard on the back wall of the garage. Yes, there it is still shining bright, that little ray of hope in the mouldy back drawers.

Settle in co-senior with your beer and your peanuts. I'll meet you quite shortly in Whitehall and Trafalgar Square.

BE UNREALISTICALLY POSITIVE

My son asked me to go to his IRB carnival. If you don't know, this is the Australian and Interstate Inflatable Rescue Boats Championship for surf lifesaving.

I didn't know, and watching my first carnival, I was in for a big surprise.

This is a thrilling sport to watch. Fingernails are bitten to the quick, and I could hear myself chanting positive affirmations for the safe return of my boy and his compadres as they negotiated the breaking waves.

At the start of the race, the team was coming in pretty much last. Co-senior thought it was going to be a bad day. Team members were downcast. I affirmed that 'it was not over till it's over'.

All opinions led to an impossible win. I poured myself a glass of champagne while watching the boat sail into victory on the crest of a magnificent wave. I was right—stupidly, impractically, and unrealistically right—and I poured myself another one to celebrate.

Now this is certainly not about being right. This is about thinking right and attracting right and affirming right and visualizing right. And guess what? 'Right' just plonks itself on the doorstep, and before you know it, the sparkle of positivity sticks and things start to happen.

Co-senior looks at me sometimes with bemusement. He is the ying to my yang. He is pragmatic and sensible and educated, so my crazy positive ideas or comments are easily repudiated based on fact, statistics, and common sense.

But hey, sometimes results are not based on common sense. Sometimes positive attracts positive. Sometimes it feels far too simplistic, but sometimes, it really works.

I don't let it stop there—I don't give up. I nurture the power of the mind and breeze through la-la land in my skippity-doo happiness. Others watch wide-eyed in their practicality and shock, as some extraordinarily positive results do just eventuate 'cause I believed and said so.

Just today I proved my point.

Parking outside a favourite spot is usually impossible. Parking spaces are a marathon away or at least a lengthy Uber journey.

Co-senior tells me to get ready for a long walk. I shut my eyes and focus on a close, available shady spot, jiggle the coins in my pocket for luck, and ping, the tail- lights of the car right beside us flash on, and we are five seconds away from sliding in.

After a wonderful evening at the theatre, our path to the parking garage is diverted through the casino. With a little nudge, I suggested to co-senior that it would be fun to place just one bet on just one number and see what happened. Co-senior raises his eyebrows advising me that wins like that just don't happen. Never daunted, I bought my one chip, I placed it on number six (my birthday of course), closed my eyes, focussed and skip, skip stop, the ball bounced and settled into number six and a beautiful, bountiful booty was dropped into my purse. I know this may sound silly, and of course, it doesn't happen all the time—but it can happen.

So, this is how my mind works...

I think it is warm when it is really numbingly cold.

I think I am thin when there is still way to go.

I think my apple pie is delicious when the pastry is soggy.

I think my car is a Ferrari when it is only good for scrap.

I think I'll get the upgrade when it's really school holidays.

I think I'll win lotto when the percentage is slim.

I think I will be my grandkid's favourite gagga.

I think that the lump in my breast is only a cyst.

I think lymphoedema is a workable condition.

I think I'm loved by all whom I meet.

I think I will finish this book and will help many others.

I think I will change lives giving back to the needy.

I think I will age, loving each dawn and sunset.

How does your mind work?

This may sound quite loopy to you, but it certainly makes daily living so much happier.

Think positive thoughts, Boomers!

Be unrealistically positive, Boomers!

It's not over till it's over, Boomers!

No, it's not over, it's just begun!

'Keep your face to the sunshine and you cannot see a shadow.'

Yes, Helen Keller, I'm with you right there.

DUMP 'EM

OK, MY LOVELIES, WE HAVE TO FACE FACTS. WE ARE NOW older.

Do we really care what people think about us?

Is our self-esteem wrapped up in little cocoons of judgement?

Do we shrivel when we don't meet others' expectations.

Do we strive to communicate with those whose interests are so very different to ours?

Are we lonely because we feel inferior when others brag about their things or their accomplishments?

Really, Boomers, who gives a wrap? We have lived long enough to know that each minute is gold, so really, why do we even consider wasting the time in striving to belong?

In my seniorship, my past 'dumpees' are numerous and, looking back, appear very seasonal. I say that as each life season attracts different friendships that are there for just a while and then slowly fade to introduce others, and that's OK.

I have also landed at the bottom of the dump, and I am sure you have too, and that also is just fine.

Did I care then? Absolutely.

Do I care now? Absolutely not.

And I am sure you feel the same way, my fellow seniors.

Some dumps are sad and hard and take time to reconcile. Others bring light as it expels the ugliness from the physical surrounds, and emotional manipulation is outed.

My very closest friend was around, it seemed, from birth. We truly loved each other through Kindy and bullying and adolescence and covert IUD insertions. Our families were intertwined, and our souls even more so. We laughed and shared and were true blood sisters.

We both married and loved each other's partners. But in the season of marriage, other friends entered the bond. Dinner dates ensued, new friends attached to old friends, marriages broke up, and new and old friends participated in the rumour mill and gossip.

In marriage break up, there are always sides.

New friend takes sides, old friend crosses the Rubicon sucked up into the situation, and boom—dumped. It hurt, but it learnt.

And that was the start of the analysis of trust.

I had a gang of boozy friends. We would celebrate in groups, each bringing their own version of inebriation and drinking late into the night, sinking down to small talk and smut. Part of the attraction was being part of a group, but my soul never soared after the evening, which was even more evident the next day while drowning a headache in greasy fries. I never understood why, after days on yachts and in extravagant surroundings, my soul was not nurtured. I realized in one-on-one contact that there was nothing in common other than drunken small talk. What, pray tell me, feeds your soul? Listening to gossip about school parents who are most assuredly dealing with the enormous stresses behind the scenes in their endeavour to save face and keep their families together? I realized that I was accepting their invitations and then cancelling just before the occasion.

My soul was repelling in protection. The pushback didn't go down well, and the invitations thinned out. The relief was immeasurable, and I gratefully moved on.

Co-senior celebrated a milestone amongst a gang of friends from all sides of the spectrum. We howled with laughter over his misdemeanours and silly situations, all sharing a closeness that is only found after many years of trust. My 'bestie' was uncomfortable that we had other 'besties' apart from her. We asked her about the most significant part of this day of friendship or of situations we had experienced together. She replied that the best part of her day was 'watching the whales catching skin cancer' on the beach she had visited in the morning. This, I might add, as she rudely flicked a charred chicken wing across the table advising verbosely to all the guests present that it was inedibly burnt. Go get!!!! Does the little yellow head of jealousy rise so viciously in friendship, or is it seriously time to take a dump?

Some friendships just need dialogue to bring back to completion. Friendships can heal if authenticity is displayed. Words interchange in anger in differences of opinion when young. Looking back in later life, it all seems so silly.

The benefits of growing up and older is that we learn to assess with our gut and are much more competent in reacting with our heads, hence, keeping friendships intact, friendships that are meaningful and friends who wish only the best for us.

It's easy to judge others.

The lessons I have learned, however, in maturity, are that people don't behave in a certain way unless they are hurting themselves.

I've learned that friendship is not based on things and wealth and the pursuit of networking success.

People are simple and yet so diverse.

Real connected communication is based on trust and acceptance and difference and diversity and debate but, most of all, it is based on love.

'All You Need Is Love'—so say the Beatles.

Happiness is ours; it is deeply embedded in ourselves. If a relationship isn't working, then my advice is just dump 'em.

As I read the other day, 'If I'm too hard to like, then quite frankly, I won't disturb you.'

I am at peace—I hope you are too.

DEATH

WHO THE HELL ARE WE KIDDING?!

We are all scared of death, even the constantly beaming religious afficionados with spirits that never seem to age.

Don't get me wrong—I *do* have a faith.

However, 'what's it all about, Alfie?'…

So, you don't ever think about dying, and then a cannonball hits—boom!

For me, it happened on a Musgrave and Watson Tour (in my teens) through Europe. I don't think the company exists anymore, so it sort of dates me.

It was one of those tours, seventeen and footloose, too many vinos, too many croissants, too many kisses, and then, looking through the misted window of a tour bus, you see the beyond and the beyond and the beyond, and it's not about now anymore—it's about life.

If there is a beyond the beyond, where actually does it all end?

I mean, what is infinity?

Is it black on black on black?

Is it a world of tiny little stars—actually billions of stars, actually some scientists believe billions of stars in a hundred billion galaxies!!!

Blows your mind, doesn't it?

These are the strange thoughts when you become a senior.

So, back to this celestial sphere with earth-orbiting satellites.

Will we someday maybe play Pacman or hopscotch and eat up or hop over these earth-orbiting satellites? Are we still people or little shiny bubbles of light or opaque wafts of gas or what? If we were still in the human form, is there enough space for us?

And heaven or hell?

I just wish that someone had had a peek on the other side and had come back to tell us all the naughty or nice that we could expect when we dissolve to dust.

Well, I suppose I will never know till it's time, so I'd better be super-duper nice on earth.

OK, so now we are having babies. I say we, but when the kids have kids, it's sort of a team effort—will come back to that in another chapter.

We are now seniors and getting closer to the other side. So, darlings, pop those babies out quickly because we want to still have time to be that embarrassing Gagga or Pappa who breakdances at your twenty-first and reminds your friends you were once acned and sort of 'hippo-y'—I mean hippy.

I watched television the other day, where a beaming lady asked me if I had bought a pair of shoes. Well, yes of course I had—aah, then there is more—no, it's not Demtel (thought they may be adding on some fishnet stockings or Canesten for mould between the toes or something just as exciting).

Well, here goes. If you spend some of your money on shoes, then you should absolutely consider spending the same dollar on funeral insurance.

Funeral insurance—this is now serious business.

Funeral insurance—that means that there definitely is going to be an end. Are you 'mad whack' (see, I do keep up with the times)?

Now, I have to plan for the biggest party that I have ever attended, and I am not even going to be there.

Sorry, kids, you sort out the funeral.

But remember...

I am the 'princess and the pea'. I have to be tucked in very tight, and it has to be neat, edges folded immaculately and very soft under the bum—my back can sometimes get sore. Remember, darlings, I went to boarding school, and bed precision is in my DNA. Bad or good habits die hard.

Good night.

REALITY TV

OK, BOOMERS, NOW IT IS TIME TO FESS UP.

We were out at dinner with friends last week discussing all and everything including each one of our television viewing habits.

My friend expounded that she hardly ever watches television, and if she does it would be 'Travels through the Cotswolds' or 'Great Train Journeys' or a 'Gardening Fair' extravaganza.

Co-senior, an academic, colludes with this view.

His favourite pastime would be to mark off interesting articles in *Time* magazine and glance up here and there under pressure to see if Persian Fairy floss has been added to the panna cotta.

Ah, but I have caught co-senior out many times as he roars in glee at a try being scored in his favourite Rugby Union or fast forwards through our planner to catch up on every sporting event since the inception of time that is now clogging any space for my programmes to be held for later viewing.

So, this is when the discussion ensued.

I love the occasional drama. I love the occasional biography. I love anything musical, but here goes…

I *do* watch reality television.

So why is this genre so lean forward?

Why does it draw us in so addictively that we even have pro-grammes on series links to make sure we don't miss a single part of the next episode?

Firstly, it is so abominably contradictory, and we all love a debate, don't we?

The media explodes in their exposure of individuals delving back into deep dark hidey holes. It sucks viewers into this, engorg-ing their brains. These little piranhas frenzy feed on morsels of untrue gossip to spit out at their next barbie and beer evening.

The cooking extravaganzas encourage a search party for the gadget packed away somewhere, as we now don't need to read the instruction manual, nor do we have to trail through YouTube.

Now we have it right in front of us as we lament at its misuse on the programme and eventual demise of blubbing heartbroken contestant.

Of course, there are the music shows where everyone's 'Got Talent'. We turn in our own response to a meaningful voice and gasp at the antics of the hundredth season of anything else that is 'talenty'.

However, it is always bemusing to find that we still haven't reached the bottom of the barrel, and there is still pretty awesome talent out there.

Downside is that we will never ever reach out for our guitar again or plug in the amplifier that has been sitting at our feet for a decade for fear of our own pitch and riffs not measuring up with what we can now hear as perfect.

Then it is even lower down the food chain.

It's when a marriage takes place without previous sight. Or a single sifting through a number of beauties and 'handsomes' to pick a partner for possible lifetime experiences. Part of one's soul gets lost in the romance, stealing our sleep and poking our hearts.

This, only to be brought sharply back to earth when we discover that this is all just a smart extension of the marketing package for the latest skin or swimwear line.

It seems like it is the fame and the glory that draws these 'auditionees' in, only to find that possibly they do really connect as they are ejected on whim to collapse into humiliating disinterest.

So, co-senior and I have an ongoing thing about the channel changer.

He surfs into the reality of world history, and I snuck back into reality of the absurd.

The ads are too loud, so he mutes when he can. When the eyes are down, I surf back to mine.

He declares loudly that reality television is inane and dumbing and uninteresting. I agree but disagree, part of a Gemini thing.

I suck up by placing a beautiful bombe alaska and duck a l'orange under his nose.

It not only buys me more time but also subtly reminds him that his Rugby Union is also reality television—just in another form.

BE FEARLESS
ABOUT YOUR FLAWS

I HAVE A CROOKED LOWER FRONT TOOTH.

This happens when you are the third child and the queen of hand-me-downs. Money is tight, older siblings have been through the whole rigmarole of orthodontic treatment, and it's now *Whatever*!

The premise is pushed that a 'squiff 'tooth is unique and different.

It has never really bothered me, and I have never really noticed it until recently. My latest grin in the mirror lost the 'sparklies' at the bottom half of the selfie. It felt like Halloween had come to visit early or I was the result of a rapid tobacco chewing 'meth' mouth.

When I feel jump-out-of-my-skin healthy, I am too loud, and when I don't feel myself, I am a hermit. Some people love the loud me. It is bees to the honey. Other people loathe it and are ready with their scythes to chop down the tall poppy invading their leadership space, which they tightly preserve in fear of usurpation.

When it is hermit time, friends call to chat. I decline graciously for them to vanish for the next six months protecting their confusion, thinking they have been barred from the loud friend they had celebrated with last night.

I have lipoedema in my legs.

You probably don't know too much about lipoedema, but it is caused by inflammatory fat deposited in just the places you don't want it to appear.

If you don't take care of it, you can balloon in a very short space of time, so the condition needs to be massaged back into place and monitored continually.

It can be painful and it's not very pretty. It caused all kinds of insecurities as an adolescent when all the other nymphets were running around in thong bikinis while I was sheathed from head to toe in a pareo spruiking the new fashion statement.

I know lots about a lot of things but don't feel like an expert at anything.

My one friend sews professionally

My other friend gardens extensively.

Yet another can recite every Shakespeare verse and

Another speaks ten languages.

I just know bits about bits and *thank you* in Greek, which is a good thing to know, but not the whole about anything.

Are you like this—a multi-talented, multi-faceted human being who loves to learn about it all?

So now I have grown up, and I now have some answers to the above.

I love my smile and my crooked tooth. I own it; I smile broadly, and it is wholly unique to me.

I love being loud and withdrawn and can see both sides of the riverbank. Isn't diversity refreshing and what we are meant to be?

The legs were unusual from a very young age. I didn't fling myself into the waves in front of all the teenage hunks, but I learned the guitar and brought it to the beach and played all the Beatle songs and attempted Pink Floyd.

Hey—presto!—it was bees to the honey once again, and I was singing in a band at a five-star hotel the next night, making friends that I kept for fifty years.

Oh, and another aside, I have another skill: I can't sink.

I can drink a cup of tea sitting in the sea with my legs crossed and have a lovely afternoon with my gurgling swim partners. Come have a cup of tea with me in the water, but stay close if you ever have to jump ship. I am a great lifesaving life raft.

So, are any of us experts out there?

I know I can play the piano and guitar and sing and make ice bowls and ice cream and use MYOB and write books and…

But I am not an expert at anything. Isn't that exciting, Boomers?

We don't have to prove ourselves to anyone.

We have the freedom to play with what we love.

It is now our time.

All this knowledge of a multitude of things can be blended into one big glorious pot creating a multifaceted stew of skills.

Give it a try.

It can only invade your souls, dear Boomers, and fearlessly push you to the other side of freedom.

DOWN DOWN DOWN UP

——

SOME DAYS ARE JUST BLAH!

We all have them.

Maybe we drank too much wine yesterday. Maybe we ate too much chocolate. Maybe our best friend is having coffee with our other best friend and we are not invited.

Maybe our grandchild said they didn't like us today.

There are those days when the sun isn't sparkling as bright as usual, the hips aren't working as nimbly as usual, the brain is befuddled in remembering details, and life is just plain ordinary.

So why today, dear Boomers, why is this day so flat?

Starting with sleep—if we don't sleep, we just get plain grumpy. The carousel about looping on different situations never stops. But it won't stop if we don't push the stop button.

Finances are tight, and maybe budgeting is delayed to prevent facing the real traumas of debt and despair.

The children are scattered around the globe, so contact is pixelated in Facebook video calls.

The discussions are fleeting, and details are scarce—never comparing with a good cappuccino in the cafe next door.

There is a lump in the breast that feels like a pea. It's not looking good, but medical insurance doesn't pay for a radiography visit to the hospital, so it's wait your turn till the breast van comes back to an accessible area.

The stairs are a nuisance as the knees are creaking, and the phone is always downstairs when you have just crawled upstairs, so it's another slog to go and fetch.

The friends are getting older and are more cautious of driving, so visits are less frequent and the hours more lonely. And some of the besties have dropped off, and we miss their frequent repetitive chats.

The eyes are more blurry, and the drops make us squint. The next step is more drastic, and that doesn't feel fun.

The startups are costly and easily discarded when the truth of investment and cash flow locks in.

The gutters need fixing, and the carpet is tattered; the quote differentials are vast, and the tradies see 'senior' and decide to rip off.

It's just a Bitch of a Day, I would say.

Two little rosellas fly over and sit on the window ledge, spectacular in their variegation. They peck at each other and look straight in my eyes.

A cockatiel squawks in the branches, and a kangaroo hops down the driveway in suburban Australia.

The clouds part, and sun's rays dance through the fleece and warm the soul.

A coffee chases the mud away, and lucidity visits.

The share market has turned, and there is a little to play with.

The breast is all cleared, and the eye drops now settled.

The grandkids are sparkling in their newly formed words and don't see the grey or the wrinkles or dentures.

And who gives a rip about the stairs and the house and the gutters? We have somewhere to live, for goodness' sake, and that is always a blessing.

Come on, Boomers, we don't have the luxury of bemoaning our languor.

Cold wash your face, slap on anti-inflammatory, and go for a walk, dear Boomers, and thank your lucky stars that you are still living and still very much alive.

ISOLATION IS COMFORTABLE BUT DANGEROUS

WE HAVE PRECIOUS FRIENDS THAT LIVE OUT OF TOWN.

We don't see them as much as we would really love to, and we make many promises that we will set a date.

By the time we do see each other, the greys have exploded, the wrinkles have progressed, and who knows we may not even recognize each other. That, mixed in with wonky knees and medicated bloodshot eyes and a hearing aid here and there.

We do, however, talk abundantly in the missing months. We know all about each other's progression into the next stages of life, and in our last conversation, we delved deeper into the reasons about this lack of physical contact.

My friend said, 'You know, Jules, I am scared of driving into the city.'

And I get it. Driving is not the same as it used to be.

Eyes are diverted to mobile phones either attached to the eardrum or hanging off dashboards with no regard for the rules or the safety or the possibility of licence loss. Everyone seems to speed, and our unhurried momentum is causing much aggression with tailgating and swerving and unsafe conditions.

Only today, a little red speedster was almost conjoined to my taillights.

I must admit, I immediately presumed it was another generation. Turning my head for a monster stare as the driver drew up side to side, knock my cotton socks off, the inhabitant of said speed bomb was on the wrong side of seventy.

'Go Granny Go'—so say the Beach Boys.

Time in the motor vehicle is spent in anticipation mode waiting to dodge someone else's mistake or keeping a monumental distance from a crazy motor cyclist or errant truck driver being remunerated by the mile. This, while swerving between motor vehicles in the quest for higher pay days.

It is almost as if there is a thrill attached to this.

No wonder my friend is frightened.

We live in the city and are used to the cautious travels, but they live amongst their animals and farm roads, and their only errant experience is an occasional cow deciding to cross the road.

Then, of course, on reaching our destination, the issues of parking rear their expensive nasty head.

Not only do we have to draw out our life savings to pay for an extended period, but we are pretty smooth about following the green light and sailing front forward into a vacant space without a pause to other impatient parkers.

Now we have to be aware of the reverse manoeuver that seems in fashion and not drive too close to cause conflict. Maybe it's a good thing that our hearing is not as proficient to hear the barrage of abuse that follows should we transgress just a little over the line.

Then the retailers sigh in desperation as we fiddle in our purses to draw out the correct coin for the newspaper.

Cash? What is that?

Nobody pays cash these days, and frustration oozes out of every pore as they wait for a millisecond while we fumble with our stiff and arthritic fingers.

So I get it.

Sometimes it's wonderful to have the groceries delivered, the dinner delivered, the friendships virtual, the computer companion, and a favourite tea bag dumped into the favourite cup midafternoon, still in the morning activewear attire.

Sometimes silence is refreshing and the lack of judgement glorious and no awareness of what's out there hallucinogenic.

But does this become too comfortable?

Is one's own silence and solitude becoming our norm, and does our brain relax into ineptitude without awareness?

Is the result of the gentle narrowing of our perimeter truncating any further growth, and do we sink into oblivion in our cosy home comfort?

I would say the effort to explode into life at any age is vital for our lifespan. Isolating ourselves through fear will not do us any favours.

Get up, get dressed, get out, get connected.

'Flip the fear and make it, in its hold on isolation, it's own plain and nervous cissy.'

(Read in a motivational book somewhere and loved)

WHAT EVERY GRANDPARENT SHOULD KNOW

MY GRANDDAUGHTER, ALL OF FIVE, RUSHED HOME THE other day to inform me that the following day was Cultural Day at her school in Los Angeles, and each student needed to take a culturally relevant dish to school to hero this tradition.

As Mumma was fully occupied with her new little arrival, it was left up to Gagga to find a solution.

Being an Australian, top of mind offering was Lamingtons. But, not being the best cookie maker (for fear of eating everything and messing up my scale figures), the whole 'roll the cake in chocolate and coconut' caused a violent mess explosion on body, hands, and face, with shrieks of delight from granddaughter that 'Gagga was the best cooker in the world'.

I quietly placed our offering on the display table at school the next day, surrounded by perfect macaroons from France, delicious samosas from India, Kourabiedes from Greece, colourful paella from Spain, and our uneven but heartfelt offering from Australia.

The Lamingtons had unfortunately been under the heavy plate carrying last night's leftovers so were somewhat squashed in their presentation.

I gently worked at coercing my little one away from the table and away from any admittance that this had come from our kitchen.

But *this* little one was having nothing to do with it, and stood steadfast, hands on hips, positioned in front of the plate, informing all parents and children who walked past that these Lamingtons were made by her Gagga, and everyone needed to sample.

Parents slid past attempting to fake delight but firmly declined imbibing.

With that, granddaughter tearfully turned to let us know that nobody was eating our Australian delight, and her confidence was fading, as well as her confidence in my honoured title of 'Best Cooker in the World'.

I was very nimble during that turn, grabbing a number of Lamingtons and passing them behind my back to co-senior who started the long journey of stuffing them into his mouth to conceal all evidence.

The plate was duly emptied, and granddaughter was no longer tearful, and justified her position as yummy provider, and I restored my reputation in her eyes as 'Best Cooker in the World'.

All was now tracking to plan between us two, which left poor co-senior's situation. This was not so good as he was now close to comatose with the sugar overload and required an appointment at the dry cleaner the next day to extricate the Lamingtons that had dug deep into the cavern of his trouser pocket, never to be found.

Grandparenting times like this don't always come easy. For some, it is just groundhog day, but for others, it is a whole new world. For co-senior and I, we had to ease into this new season.

Having both had children of our own on coupling, and bringing our children into the union as a package deal, we had been surrounded by children from day dot in this relationship and so were uncontrollably rather excited about a late, very late Granny gap year, enjoying kids-free zone for just a little while longer.

Our little people now, however, are the gold in our family portfolio. We love their differences and eccentricities. We love them all differently at different times, and we are mean multitaskers at nappy changing time, many times using hands as utensils to catch vagrant flow.

We have learned along the way, and—*Eureka!*—our grandchildren in our care are still alive. We have done things our way in silence sometimes, and we stay close to the rules in others. All has helped in the journey of love and care, but instinct usually rules the day.

When one of my mummies and babies came to visit at the early stages of grandparenthood, I learned my first hard lesson.

It's not wise to comment on baby's diet, even if it is beans and salmon.

My only advice is to be armed and prepared with cleaning materials at the ready as the immature palette expels and erupts. And a good deodorizer comes in very handy.

In anticipation of being wonderful grandparents, co-senior and I visited a grandparenting class at the hospital nearby. The participants were feeling slightly intimidated in expectation of their new little arrivals. We shared stories of 'when we' and were becoming more confident in our ability to keep the status quo calm.

Our lecturer advised us that 'Why don't you do it this way' needed to be rapidly erased for 'Where are you at and where can I help'. First good lesson in notes on our iPhones.

Firstly, there is a name to be chosen for 'grand-mere' of the family.

There are lots of Nannas and Grandmas and Grannies and Grammys around, but in this day and age of massive comical choices, why can't we also go rogue?

Some kid's names describe the direction, some kid's names can be eaten, some would pass as any gender, and some hipster names (i.e., Fedora, Chia, Insta, and Kale) can be worn, eaten, or viewed.

Gravity, Luna, Pilot, and Rocket transport to outer space and their progeny is right on track for *outer* outer space with Photometric Redshift and far outer space MACS0647-JD.

So, whoopee, there is lots of scope here to go trendy with the name.

Be careful of the other Grandma, if there is another, as Big Granny and Little Granny could offend.

However hard the coercion with little tongues, unfortunately they will probably work out their own version of name attachment.

For me, I became Gagga. Hopefully, the 'marked by wild enthusiasm, infatuated and doting Gagga' and not the crazy, foolish version. And then again, Lady Gaga is a star, so it puts me by name in the same hemisphere, and I'll take that.

The big day arrives to meet the new little one, and the urge to be familial doula erupts.

My mum, being a doctor's wife, barged into the birthing room, while I grunted and groaned and screamed profanities at her for not being sensitive. She left dejected and never came to visit again in the hospital, so lesson learned. Now I am in that space.

Your daughters-in-law and daughters may not like the muscular part of their genitals in full display or the disturbing of vibrational crystals and birth hypnosis app. They want you there but not too close, just close enough to cry together when hearing the first cry.

New mummas love help. They love a cup of tea or an hour's sleep or a rinse of the breast pump.

The 'drop in as I am in the area' won't work, as their hooded eyes may have just descended into the pillow.

A chicken soup does the trick or a hand with baby number one who has now become a monster at the intrusion in their cocooned world really, really does the trick. Let new mumma set the tone, and discipline is only kept for emergencies.

I am an expert now in unicorns, lost dummies, pillow under the arm baby hold.

I can interpret a squeak from a yell and whether it's rumbling tummies or a bad dream.

I know all about dinosaurs and cars and most definitely *Paw Patrol*, *The Lion King*, and the *Wiggles*.

Nappies are sometimes a fail, as they undo and make messy.

Elsa from *Frozen* is a good 'on repeat' solution.

Always have wipes — everywhere.

A good burp is a good problem solver.

Don't put the pumped breast milk in an ordinary container next to the real milk.

Routines work wonders.

And then again, when all else fails and you collapse in fatigue, there is always 'hide and seek', and for last resort, when *all* all else fails, there is always slime.

CAN ABYSS

Our beloved Jerome.

He was the beautiful strong Zulu man who was part of our family for as long as I can remember.

Jerome lived above the swimming pool pump house in an eclectic lair, swirling in marijuana vapes with us curious little girls sneaking up the iron stairs to peep into this den of iniquity.

We knew nothing wrong.

We never understood that his permanent red eyes, poor muscle coordination, and delayed reaction times were not the effects of sluggishness and apathy but a symptom of consumption to endure the long days of being a black African in an absurdly unfair environment.

That for us was the first touch point—we were just little girls, and we loved him.

We were '60s kids, and it's a miracle that so many of us survived.

Cigarettes would constantly hang from our lips. This was everywhere, and I mean everywhere—in planes, in restaurants, in beds. Parents exposed us to secondhand smoke. Cheroots hung from the lips of elegant, fur-clad ladies, and smoking jackets were donned to end an evening filled with conversation and friendship. It was regarded as a sign of maturity and oh so sexy.

Dagga vapors, as we called it, were just an extension of this hazy environment as our experimental generation floated around in caftans and minis. It was universally out there and voraciously imbibed, and our parents instilled in us that it was downright *bad*.

They educated us in the notion that this dagga, marijuana, cannabis would cause long-term or permanent change in our brains. They force-fed our guilt that we would all end up cognitively impaired and our little brain cells would pop into oblivion at just the moment in life that we needed them most.

Funny that they didn't mention the implosion of our arteries after melted ghee and lamb fat that launched the searing of our evening meal.

We didn't really take notice of their advice. We were too busy drinking water from garden hoses, wearing no sunscreen, running around barefoot, and 'passengering' beltless in the back seat of our parents' car.

Back to Jerome.

We thought he had come into the money and bought himself a new fragrance.

We didn't think much of it. It was dark and skunky. It was the scent of marijuana cleaved to his working overalls.

And so, we floated through the '60s and '70s—a perpetual 'summer of love'.

We wafted through an orgy of experiment in our happy-place heaven, assailing our bodies with foreign immigrants. Smoking this herb became our languid rebellion while trying to navigate through this cultural war.

Amid growing up, we faced the Cuban Missile Crisis and the expectation of nuclear war. JFK was gunned down, and if we were on the path to annihilation, then why not implode in the haze of social experiment.

This magic herb could calm our anxieties and ease our muscles and stresses, while the world decided whether we would have the chance to peek into the future—our future.

We were not all despondent junkies, just antiestablishment groupies smoking weed en masse, lost in the maze of adolescent exploration. And all of this was illegal.

Today we are all stressed differently.

We struggle with information overload, we juggle family and financial pressures, we grab fast food as we rush to our next multitask; we breathe in polluted air as highways thread their way in and out of our suburbs.

Blood pressures and cholesterol are high, diabetes and weight gain explosive, social human contact via device and spinning out of control.

And now, after hiding our adolescent vices, we are told hang on now, alcohol will confuse and muddle the brain far faster than this wonderful new powerful word *cannabidiol*. This is just one of the compounds in the cannabis plant, but hey, it does appear to produce significant changes in the body with larger-than-life medical benefits.

It appears to calm down those nasty little inflammatory spots, relieving stiffness and pain and guess what—also chronic pain.

Mice and rats are circling on their carousels without a care in the world.

Smokers are reducing their addictions.

Epilepsy is receiving good therapeutic results.

And this little green leaf with its anti-seizure properties is providing hope in the research into its potential for fighting the dreaded C.

Anxiety is now becoming still.

The pancreas is soothed.

Acne is smoothing.

And research and studies are working overtime to establish if this is really real or the subsequent result of inhaling too much in our youth.

I would say the former as I watch the share market sit up and take notice and investors dumping life savings into the notion that cannabis is here to stay.

I return to my dearest Jerome, who smoked this illicit weed to forget about his marginalized African existence.

We shared in his ever-generous munchies while he laughed in his mind-altering state, buffering his brain from the assault on discrimination.

We were good little girls and goody-good adolescents, as I have to admit I have never smoked the weed.

But boy oh boy, things are about to change as I crawl into my car and drive off to purchase CBD oil in a pursuit to jump back into the car to race home to make love and not war on my body.

NIGHTTIME
RITUALS

MY MUMMA...

Her nighttime rituals were solidly embedded.

It was always two scotches—'can't fly on one wing', she would say.

Johnnie Walker was her warm, familiar bedtime companion, even more so when my dad was no longer around. Traitors we were if we did not 'quaff', and many a night we would dizzy up to bed thinking 'holey moley, thish is one helleva eighty-year-old'.

It brought back memories of the days in our youth when we indulged the same way, partying late into the early hours and creeping into family homes, crawling up stairs, praying to remain invisible and collapsing onto the bed or whatever felt solid to sink into oblivion with alcoholic pins and needles tickling our consciences.

Those were the days!

A vino bottle was only the start of the night, and the prospect of fallout the next day not too calamitous.

We were young and fit and our livers were at their best. The four-wheel drive sitting on the frontal lobe the next morning was easily rectified with greasy egg and bacon, and if that didn't work, quick finger flick down the throat would remedy it all with a multicoloured stomach expulsion. We were good again and primed to start all over at the next celebration.

Well, back to Mum…

At eighty, the liver is not really at its best, and little sips perform the same as bottles in those days. This nightly 'Drunken Granny' ritual can take its toll, though.

Oops, I may have to rephrase—I think 'Drunken Granny' could be a porn site.

So rather than exhibiting sissy behaviour in front of our matriarch, we would clink our glasses with hearty cheers, *gesundheit, proost, salud* or whatever made her happy, with no awareness from her that our crystals were loaded up with ginger ale—thank goodness of the same hue.

Now we are edging closer to our own nighttime rituals.

Why is it such a ritual?

It's almost not worth going to bed, as there is so much to do.

We have to factor in time to make sure we are not asleep before we are asleep.

In days of yore, we could have gone to bed with mascara still on, even better, a Chanel mascara, and to wake up in the morning as Aerosmith was considered to be quite kinky.

Now, if we leave mascara on, even if we have remembered to put it on, mascara residue results in a visit to the doctor as we are quite oblivious that the brush has been sitting in the makeup drawer for ten years and has grown some nasty little offspring which are now sitting in our eyes, which we can't see out of and require some heavy disease-fighting drops to rectify.

Then, talking about eyes, we have to remove contact lenses before beddy-byes.

Our eyes are now so dry that they play hide and seek behind the eyelids, and our fingers are now shaking from lack of sleep and can't grab onto the lens.

We play hide and seek till it's way past bedtime, and we have to wake up co-senior to fiddle and faddle to get it out.

Oh, and while we do that, we have to remember to put in the prescription eye drops for optic pressure, and we can't remember which box to use as we put them all in the fridge and they have been moved. We take a chance that the eyeball won't explode in the night as we use the old stuff that we forgot was in there.

Then, hey presto, we remember that we had put the new pre-scription in another fridge and now we can't use it as we can't double dose on the drops.

Oh, and tablets, we normally have a routine of 'take after dinner'. But I think in our distant memory, we took the tablets earlier as they were just sitting there and we didn't want to forget.

And now, we forget if it was tonight or last night, and co-senior has filled my bottle where I was measuring my water intake, and I can't assess whether I have drunk out of the bottle to take the tablets.

So—dilemma!—do I take the tablet again and will I be dial-ing 000 and rushed to emergency for a stomach pump because there is now too much in the bloodstream?

Or do I not take it and risk a rush of 'bad stuff' flooding my bloodstream as I obliviously lie in slumber?

So counting down—we forgot to make the bed this morning, so even though we are stiff and tired it has to get done. For co-se-nior, he could sleep on a plank and nothing would bother him. For me, boarding school was my ruination.

How can you sleep with a crease under your left toe with the ridge irritating all night and the seam in the doona needs to be straight, not an inch over?

So, who is checking, one would ask oneself?

My body is checking; it just can't go to sleep.

So, at last it is bath or shower time.

The bath needs to be just right coz the shower is wrong. The shower floor is always cold, so standing there in one's vulnerability produces only cold toes, and then you can't sleep as the blood won't spread to these far-off lands and hangs around the head to give that little extra boost to the hot flush. The head is in summer, and the toes are in winter, and both compete with the cool pillow and warm blanket for supremacy on the bed.

Well, it just means no sleep, zilch, naught.

Counting backward doesn't work, Arianna Huffington's advice on sleep doesn't work, meditation doesn't work, or maybe…

Oh, damn, I forgot to brush my teeth, and my mouth splint is in another room. Now I will have to get up and get it 'cause my neck is out from writing, and I will grind my amalgam filling into the jawbone if I don't.

And then, one more bathroom visit just in case and

Phew!!! I can now go to sleep.

At last the day is done, but holy shit, when I wake up in the morning I hope I can remember that once again I have to go through the whole process — only this time, it is all in reverse.

IT'S THE DISASTERS IN LIFE THAT BRING OUT OUR BEST

I WAS A LEAD SINGER IN A BAND AT THE BUDDING AGE OF thirteen.

It wasn't really planned, just a result of group guitar singsongs on the beach led by *moi*, guitar curves hiding my own.

Before I knew it, I was on stage with four gorgeous boys, and my parents listened to my voice echo across the valley knowing as soon as it stopped, it was time to race down the hill to collect me before the ravishers of teenagehood took over.

My father complained loudly that I was turning night into day and day into night, of which the punishment was early morning disciplinary wakeups to walk the endless eighteen-hole golf course in the suburb close by.

My band occurrence became a yearly pilgrimage, and the anticipated new material to practice and perform at the end of the year was unbearable as I ran over barefooted to the hotel to see if 'my boys' had arrived.

The bond of friendship was unbreakable, even to the extent of my poor dad, once again, being manipulated into driving me into the 'back of beyond' to spend school holidays with their family.

It was unwise to think of forming a more intimate relationship with my favourite boy, even though at that age teenage hormones were exploding, and sometimes I wished for nothing more. Our group gift of singing was too valuable, and nobody wanted to break this magic circle and disband the perfect harmony.

Having attended an all-girls boarding school, formal time was a very stressful time for some. The uninitiated sidled up to school friends to seize their brothers as partners, and when these contacts ran out, the invitations were extended to the outer circle of friends.

Of course, I was sitting pretty; I had my band of brothers and so was quick to invite my 'bestie boy' to attend as my friend's partner.

Formal day arrived, but partner did not.

My schoolfriend was embarrassed. I was disappointed.

I knew this behaviour was not consistent with the person I knew. I knew he would never let my friend down and would never, never let me down.

In the early hours of the morning, *that* call came through.

The accident was caused by someone else exiting a driveway without caution.

My friend in the backseat was trapped in the carnage, and all that was left of his 'before' was eye movement with a single tear proving that he was still alive amidst this feeling of nothingness.

I jumped on a train and rushed to his side.

He told me that he had had a huge quarrel with his father, and when he woke from unconsciousness, he apologized to his dad for not doing anything right.

I remember that moment fifty years on.

It taught me to never wallow in unresolved conflict.

It taught me to apologize before it was necessary.

It taught me that things change in a minute and music and the music of life can lapse into abject disharmony from cruel unexpected events.

I learned so many lessons from this boy who grew to a man.

He gained movement to his waist, and even though he lost his brawn, he never allowed himself to lose his brain.

He competed in paraplegic sports festivals.

He qualified as a lawyer.

He married and had two beautiful boys.

He travelled all over the world.

He ran his own magazine company.

He never looked back.

I lost touch with him for a number of years as our lives catapulted in different directions, in different cities, and in different countries.

It was not until one of his employees asked for leave to attend a wedding and on discussion they ascertained that it was my wedding that we re-established our connection and I learned about his achievements.

We had known each other as children and now laughed again as adults.

I spoke to him at length before his operation and spoke again just before he left forever to run unencumbered through the pattern of clouds.

I hear his music today, and it floods my memory.

It reminds me of bravery and accomplishment and beauty and love.

It informs me that life with a spinal cord injury is still worth living for those who want to do so.

It teaches me tolerance in sweating the small stuff, where he had to embrace a completely different life.

Even though my inspiration could no longer play Clapton on his guitar, his example of heroic acceptance could never stop the music.

THE TASTE, SOUND, AND SMELL OF MEMORY

—

It's Valentine's Day, and co-senior and I are eating Italian in aptly named Trastevere. We are devouring spaghetti bolognaise and a robust red while holding hands, blended with deep and guttural laughs.

The familial nose of the wine invades our spirits, bringing back intense nostalgia of the days in our twenties, engulfed in amour on a Saturday date — co-senior mouthing, 'I'll meet you anytime you want in our Italian restaurant'. (Thank you, Billy Joel.)

This Trastevere is actually the name of the restaurant in Los Angeles, not the charming medieval neighbourhood with vibrant nightlife in the glorious Italian city of Rome.

But the ever popular ragù, however, has diffused itself over worldwide tastebuds, and its aroma of tomato and oregano are deeply embossed in the deliciousness of our memories.

I sit with my love on this day, our eyes and hearts deeply connected.

The taste of love has opened the door, and I am home.

✻

Crème brûlée—it's that creamy, melt-in-your-mouth taste sensation that shouts out more! while the deep engrained calorie counter ticks over heftily. It screams of indulgence and marathons to negate.

This Trinity cream French innovation is always first off the mark when it comes to after-dinner guilt choice. It is always found on the cruise menu, the restaurant stalwarts, and the home cook's repertoire. Its creaminess hums on the tongue, and the taste buds beg for more.

It was my mum's 'star offering'. She was the doyen of crème brûlée, the queen of cream and king of crackle. As children, we could choose our birthday meal, and crème brûlée always won the comp. We would wait expectantly, spoons raised to crack in harmony and familial unison.

Today, as the creamy river of custard and sugar tickles my hippocampus (a fancy name for the part of the brain that remembers episodes), I am sitting way back deep in my memory cracking the surface merrily, while at the same time cracking up at each one of our family members' inner jokes.

The taste of family welcomes me home.

Sardines and condensed milk! Yes, just exactly that. Pretty 'ew' in description but oh so magnificent in its contribution to boarding school midnight feasts.

It had all the elements of subterfuge and hidden tins surreptitiously revealed in midnight liaisons and the munch of sweet and fishy in alternates while giggling in dormitory cubicles.

Friendships were formed in huddles of motif pyjamas, and nobody cared about the frequent explosive bathroom visits the next morning when the stomach welcomed this nasty combination.

There was no awareness from our part of fish aroma slathered over elite bedding for our dormitory monitors to find or the sideways glances from teachers searching in bins to remove the odour of remnants of a day-old lunch box.

Today I have matured in my taste separation. I mash sardines with lemon on toast and lick a condensed milk spoon to complete. The memory of sound of my friends' hushed giggles rekindles the friendships and takes me back to being young and playful and included and thirteen years old, and the taste of friendship warms my soul.

Measles is nasty but even nastier when the hot summer African sky explodes with arrows of vengeance making a direct hit on the roof of our thatched family home.

Pandemonium ensued.

My dad and brother and helpful neighbours clambered up ladders, grabbing thatch from the roof to hurl onto concrete below in their futile endeavor to save what eventually disintegrated to cinders.

The flames crackled, the smell of smoke engulfed, and my little inflamed body enveloped in 'rashy' disease now added soot and grime to the pattern. It felt like hell had knocked on the door as we watched our security crumble while huddled in odor-filled blankets. The orange and red flames taunted while burning the vision into our memories and olfactories.

There is something about smoke that pervades.

It pervades from back burning and winter warming, but that day it pervaded my little girl memory and hung in my hair and environment for days.

Smoke now to me anxiously returns to that moment, delving back into memory and portends unrealistic calamitous disaster at the very first distant whiff. I feel that intensity of recall as Australia struggles to protect its land in the blazing summer infernos.

✳

I was brought up in a medical family, hence the desire to question absolutely every drug that passed my lips. As a toddler, anaphylaxis as a result of sulfur drugs had scarred my memory. Hence every medication, however harmless, was an almighty PTS experience.

As a doctor's daughter, we were always the guinea pigs for outdated pharmaceutical samples that were stored at the rear of the mirrored bathroom cupboard. The inept medication was just as ruthless as the lack of sympathy in a medical family to just get on with it in our quest to get better.

As the third child, I was shunted from parent to parent juggling between work and family life. One parent would remove me while the other enthusiastically embraced their space. Routines became imperative to keep things tight.

One of these routines was the regular Sunday 'rounds' with my brilliant surgeon father to visit his recuperating patients and spread a little joy in their recovery. There was always the offer of boiled candy-striped 'sweets' that were joyfully stashed away in their sticky glory while the wounded and bloody limbs faced off at exactly eye level for a little girl.

The nasal passages breathed in the odour of congealed blood and antiseptic. I still smell it today when walking the white corridors of death and healing. It gives me the shivers as it churns up the past, and a whiff of raw flank in the butcher's window invades the senses, indelibly etched in my brain.

Despite the horrors of medical rounds, there were always rewards at the end of the journey.

A quick halt at the local cafe brought home treasures for the day.

For my dad it was Turkish delight, for myself a Crunchie bar, and for my mum a slab of dark chocolate.

As her offering was larger than ours, I was allowed just a tiny nibble, handed out as a peace offering for shelving me out.

I eat that tiny piece of chocolate these days, let it richly dissolve on my tongue, enjoy the taste of memory, and know 100 percent why I never became a doctor.

Divorce is ugly and sad and empty.

I know. I have been there.

It seems like a lifetime ago, and I sometimes think was it really me when I look at co-senior, who has been the love of my life for forty-five years.

The pain of discovery of unfaithfulness breeds the seeds of mistrust in all relationships and makes me considerably more cautious in letting the walls crumble to form endearing forever friendships.

I was blindsided in divorce and questioned whether it was from fatigue or new 'mothership' or overweight pregnancy residue that resulted in my ex's quick dash into the arms of his secretary.

I begged for attention and love and came to the final realization that I was probably just fat. A visit to the newsagent was the remedy to rectify this.

It only took the purchase of a twenty pack of menthol mind-blowing cigarettes to commence the journey of deflation. I knew from reading countless articles that this was the quick-start method for dropping weight, and then I would be loved again.

I recall sitting amongst the trees and spring blossoms, lighting up number one to number twenty, all in quick succession, as I walked through the haze of an unpredictable future and pervading smoke-filled branches—the odour rancid as sewers, dancing through the freshness of blossoming spring flowers.

I gag today at that smell, running away from its fetid aroma into the promise of spring and beautiful future days. The distant whiff of cigarettes, even to this day, brings back the decay of divorce, and I don't want to visit too often.

*

I was six months pregnant and the decision to fly overseas to Portugal for a baby moon seemed perilous in recollection these days. I was a sizeable six monther, my toes were already eclipsed, and the overseas flight was spent in perfuse apology to my airplane neighbour who had to succumb to flesh osmosis on his side of the armrest.

This little sojourn, moving into the last months of pregnancy, was impulsive at best.

Co-senior was prepped and ready for any dramas with me, gallantly lifting my burgeoning luggage on and off travelators while I stood back in my developmental glow.

Co-senior, however, wasn't prepped, while heaving my accoutrements, for the sudden crotch rip of his trousers and the instantaneous burst-through of multi-patterned Bonds undies and well-cocooned man package.

A frantic search for the travel sewing pack—minus scissors for border security rules—ensued, and with the discovery of only one needle, one pin, and black and white cotton, we twosome dashed into the disabled bathroom to tack some respect into the flaying trousers.

I have to admit I have never been a competent seamstress, so with broad inexperienced strokes, positioned the needle through and out, with co-senior in Big Toe Yoga pose, needle skimming very close to the 'diddy wops' and co-senior wincing at every move.

Job was completed in haste as the last call for our flight echoed over loudspeakers, the black cotton adding interesting applique detail to beige trousers.

We strode out of the accessible toilet with our dignity intact—well, maybe not completely intact—as accusing eyes followed our every move, imagining some perverse coupling amongst the bathroom walls. This was corroborated in full by the strange gait of co-senior as he manoeuvered his way around undies and package that had been caught up in the rumble and were now firmly attached to the lining of his mono, now patterned, travel trousers.

We did make the flight, and we did arrive in Portugal, but we didn't receive our luggage. This is not the perfect situation at six months pregnant, arriving on holy weekend and staying with friends.

We could cry or just live, and we chose the latter, spending the next two days in my friend's nightie, as nothing else fit and no shops were open, sitting cross-legged in front of their winter fire indulging in caldo verde and Bacalhau and the mouthwatering offering of 'melt in your mouth' pastéis de nata.

Natas—those creamy, custardy, lemony, crunchy moreish taste sensations of Portuguese custard tarts. As I sit in a cafe today with co-senior forty years later and crunch into my first bite, the custard oozes onto my tongue, and I linger in the hope that the taste remains.

I return to the feeling of warmth and friendships and living, and I cherish that there are all kinds of tastes and smells and sounds that take me back to precious moments, but today especially, flavour my brain in nostalgia.

WHY DO BOOMERS GO SHORT?

When I turned the big three-oh, my closest girlfriend told me that this was the cutoff age for the 'cut off' hair.

It was time to go short.

Funny, I thought, as it was just the reverse for the boys (are we allowed to say *boys* these days, or do we just play 'guess the gender'?). This demographic was thinking in reverse and grew theirs even longer, accessorizing with beautiful long beards. They got even fancier with a ponytail or two and a stud here and there.

My friend, however, informed me that shorter hair was a sign of glamorous maturity. All now needed to be neat with no blow your hair back in the wind status. The 'short' cut commanded respect, and a long-exposed neck was the first step in other things to come. Long hair was simply unruly and carried a strong alliance to ailing bank balances and limited education.

I consoled myself that she was just jealous. Her mass of thin fibres demanded constant attention, and the short bob was luckily her escape route to only a very occasional wolf whistle. My fibres, on the other hand, were late maturers and had come into their own in a wavy mass of expansive curls, attracting plentiful notice.

I bucked her advice and remained long—I mean, Faye Dun-away—mmm mmm.

Longer hair has no expiration date.

It will tell you when it's time for the chop.

Haircuts give me PTS.

My mother thought it was neat to be short and tidy. It was the pudding bowl look that did it for her. It was boringly short, bland, and boyish. This look only lasted until the age of consent. I threw a tantrum and consented no more, and the pudding bowl was gone. PTS, though, remained after a hairdresser up north decided that a trim should be well above the ears, resulting in a rebellious curly army just waiting for the rain and humidity to expand exponentially. I hid in my humility under hats and in bands until I could 'out' again feeling more like me.

The blow dry is a simple first base. This is followed closely by chemical straighteners that shred the scalp to leave wispy dry ends. This takes a lifetime to renew while devouring all the life savings. We were brash and brave then and embraced the creative as we sometimes exploded in rainbows as well, keeping pace with new and different trends.

Then, the ironing board had a go with our locks, sliding flat between two dampish dish clothes for fear of singe. The result *was* dead straight, but the aroma of burns invaded the nostrils, and the smell of yesterday's beef on the dish cloth aromatically blended into a cacophony of fragrance.

Colour was the next creative stage. After beer and lemon conditioner, we slathered it on with our heads hanging over bathtubs. We were individuals, were we not, but ended up quite ordinary in our sameness. Bright copper red stained the porcelain of the bath prompting the uninitiated to think foul play had taken place. Bright red worked for some but stood in its aloneness without the association of freckles.

Black was ghoulish but frightened off the unwanted. Blonde was sexy to attract the b…b.. b….boys. Well, not all the boys, just the Marilyn adulators.

Now we don't give a rat's if our hair sits in sparse spikes or hangs in plaits to our knees — or we shouldn't.

Long hair — don't care!!!

Colour sits on the scalp to fill in the spaces, and we buy little pencils and brushes and 'goodymajiggies', which we dump into hair paint and drown in respiratory impairment as we swirl hair lacquer around our head. We love the 'grandies' twirling what we have left. We love wearing bows and bands even if the family thinks we've gone 'gagga', but most of all, we are damn glad we have got hair at all.

And finally, a final word about short. Are we all getting shorter?

My midis are now hanging to the floor.

My tops are drooping in body sympathy, and bra straps pop out to say hi in all the gaps that appear. The shoulders have decided to move closer to greet each other more snugly, and co-senior and I are almost eye level when he used to be tall.

Co-senior agrees with me that it is all getting short, including our patience and, sometimes, our bank balance.

Well, let's just be positive, there is less body to worry about, and so what if we are now small. It's just the world that has become so big.

SO, WHAT DO YOU DO?

Co-senior and I were socializing last week. We don't socialize as much these days, as we now no longer have our business, and much of the socializing incorporated work parties and motivational cocktails.

Things are different now.

The business was part of our DNA, part of our wake up in the morning, and concluding this part of our life was traumatic. We made the decision suddenly, and our brains and lifestyle had no time to catch up. Impulsive five-star dinners are now a rarity, and dollars in the bank watched more circumspectly, allowing now for the occasional treat and not the historical frivolity of spending.

In this time of change, we find that we both love our space but both love being together—such a conundrum but very workable. *Thank God*, I say to myself, as I read about couples who have nothing to say to each other when the kids fly the nest or when the partner returns to the nest.

Trips to supermarkets are now tandem experiences, and 'Are you OK?' echoes through the walls when we hear unusual bangs. Visions of broken limbs or cracked skulls implode in our twenty-four-seven coupling brain as we 'step at a time' crawl downstairs to see all is still in order and working.

It sounds bad, but it really isn't. We are now called *seniors* — wtf — but that doesn't mean we are done. Our brains are still ticking overtime, and we have much still to experience and learn and explore. These two bodyworks are not going to lie down without a fight.

We are told that retirement is the new promotion, and 'when we get this, Boomers, we are free'.

Haven't we all slogged away for countless years, some of us answering to individuals up the chain, titillating their every whim? Or maybe some of us have held court as commander in chief, directing the avenues of corporate life with our expertise while dubiously embracing the fact that 'uneasy lies the head that wears the crown' (so says King Henry IV in Shakespeare's masterpiece).

And then we are 'retired'.

Don't know if I really like the term.

Who or what 'retires' us?

Does it mean we are retired to seclusion as we withdraw from our occupation or position?

Is it age, is it creaky bones, is it a slower brain, hence the fear of making mistakes?

Or is it our choice, completely, expectantly, and deliciously?

I would rather use the term 'rewired'. We are not redundant, for goodness' sake, or ceased. We refuse to fall into the abyss of loneliness and nothingness. This is just another milestone, another planting for harvest. We are not apparitions of nothingness.

Who is the smarty pants who even thinks to put us in this category? At last we have the time to do what we really want to do, what makes us happy. At last we are not afraid to be free and to have the nerve to believe that we can and will do just that.

Co-senior and I love rattling around together. However, just show us a party or celebration and we are all in, dancing on the counters if our wonky knees would let us and not worrying about any inappropriate conversation. We can always plead aged ignorance if we push just a little too far over the line.

And then the question is asked at these gatherings:

'So, what do you do?'

Seems to always be a convenient throwaway conversation startup line. I rather like that we are still considered to be 'doing' something. I told you we look and feel and act twenty years younger, therefore the question seems quite natural.

So, what do I do, I ask myself?

The reply used to be 'I run my own business, and I wake up at 6 a.m., very early, to tackle the traffic and collapse into bed way after midnight after completing my accounting tasks that have piled up over the past year.'

Does that sound like a good day to you?

'I never have a holiday, and I never see my friends, and I am exhausted all the time'(said sotto voce).

That sentence seems like a very long day.

That was me, well defined, successful, busy and relevant.

Is there a smidgeon of self-worth attached to what I said I did?

Today I pause, but only for a second, and answer loud and clear.

You want to know what I do?

I no longer confuse my 'do' with my 'who'.

I now do exactly as I please.

I dance, strip, work, sleep, swim, laugh, learn, explore exactly what I want to do and when I want to do it.

I am ever so excited that my self-worth is measured by me now coz I don't give a damn about what others think, and I will never again measure me by the false identity that what I do is so important that it has become who I am.

THE THREE-DAY RULE

CO-SENIOR SAYS WE SHOULDN'T STAY WITH PEOPLE, AND people shouldn't stay with us.

Well, let's be really specific. He does say there is an exception: if it is only for three days, but after that it's sort of like fish—there is a distinct aroma. Sorry to say I agree with him—the thought of three days of constant meal preparation, and after 'catch up', the third day of small talk makes me want to exit rapidly on a jet plane to anywhere.

I think it's because it takes so much longer to kick-start the engine. There is so much more to do in the morning these days—contact lenses take forever, dressing is more laboured, hair is uncontrollable, and let's not forget ablutions, which are a trickier problem without the prune juice forgotten last night, and the vagrant black hair growing straight above the cupid's bow.

So when did that unfriendly visitor decide to rear its head?

My beautiful elderly mum was vigilant in her family visits and always with good intention. However, her day plan was on the other side of the universe to ours. In those days we had a young family with responsibilities of a new school-shoe purchase and homework and daily scheduled routine.

For her, it was about 'tour guide' taking her on trips to every conceivable tourist spot and 'shooting the breeze' over countless glasses of Scotch.

About the Scotch, that is another story.

Mum's customary habit of two Scotches every night made sure that she never flew on one wing. Co-senior was now under the spell of daily inebriation, which was rapidly disrupting his judgement and attacking his liver.

The only solution was doubling up on poor Mumma, so shut-eye came much earlier. Ginger ale, as mentioned before, was a good mimic for co-senior. He was thankfully still in full control of his functioning marbles, while Mumma was fuzzily tucked into bed.

That was those days, and now those days are now days as we slip into seniorship and enthusiastically visit family who live all over the world.

Picture us in the USA—do we or don't we thwart the three-day rule? In seniorship we are more aware of the distribution of savings, and what the hell, surely family stays work for all, as kids say 'Hi, Mum, bye, Mum', while little people snuggle and dribble into our layers of indulgence, happily drinking in the familiarity of smell and love.

My God, it is such a responsibility.

What if they fall?

What if they choke?

What if they scream?

What if they drown?

What if we collide?

What if they roll down the stairs?

What if we forget the school snacks?

It's monumental!!!

There are strict rules in being a senior 'rellie'.

Kids of millennials are reasoned with, never spanked, choose their dinner, and if it is not to their liking, it is a successive attempt to placate hungry little tummies and angry little minds.

It's matcha and houmous and berries and almond yoghurt and always, always — did I say *always* — gluten-free. It's big, big trouble if a cupcake slips into the repertoire, even worse with sprinkles on top, and even even worse if coloured sprinkles on top. This is a total mandate for primitive shenanigans, prostrate 'tanties' and sleepless, tearful nights, and always remember — it's always about reasoning and never, no never, a spank. Yes, I know that that was our form of punishment and it is what we knew best, but I agree we wouldn't hit each other, so why would we hit a frustrated juvenile?

Driving with these nippers is also a challenge.

Picture it. We drive on the other side of the road, and 'littlie' has had a long day at school. We know as she runs to the car with her kids Jelly Beams' light up sneakers vividly flashing, beautifully fastened on the incorrect foot. She roars as the snack box contains healthy rather than sugar-loaded and stuffs her mouth with the salty popcorn while at the same time playing darts with the little white bubbles that land in co-senior's hair and fly past my ears rather like genetically modified bumblebees.

The trip home is tense.

For co-senior, it's because Bossy Bertha next to him is frantically right-hand waving to avoid collision, and Baby Bean has found the window button and is singing 'Staying Alive' as she tries to show her clambering and Houdini skills to climb out of her seatbelt and the window.

If you are a senior 'rellie', you have tasks in the 'rellie' household.

Co-senior's job is walking the dogs.

Sometimes it's a little cheat as he walks them on the lead around the yard. Other times his responsibility is taken very seriously with a long hike for said pets to exhaust and prevent countless poo pickups on return. It is a long scoot as the cracks in the pavement present considerable anxiety in one low-sighted pooch.

The family live in a celebrity-centric environment complete with tourist open vans driving up and down ready for a glimpse of the last Oscar winner. These same tourists are poised expectantly, mesmerized by the environment, cameras cocked, eyeballs glued, and — *Geronimo!* — they see co-senior, mistaken for Bruce Willis, and launch their flashes just as low-sighted pooch launches a huge, runny, steaming doodoo right in front of a beautiful brand-spanking-new Tesla with co-senior exasperatedly shouting, 'For goodness sake, Charlie, not in front of a Tesla!!!' Now isn't Facebook and Instagram going to look original tomorrow — I mean even Bruce Willis' dog poops!!!

And bees!

After one of the so-called yard walks, a bee decided to join the family as the door was firmly shut. The door needs to be firmly shut, actually, as one of the pooches went for his nightly ablution and was pounced upon by a coyote. It was horrid being a senior 'rellie' in a house full of heartbreak, but experience tells us that things happen for a reason, and it could have been the new baby.

Did I mention that there is a new baby in the house, and a bee flying around the house uncomfortably close to the baby's room sends tremulous shivers down the spine? At least the door is shut, but bees sting, and it hurts.

Co-senior is now flying around the kitchen with a dishcloth trying to seek and destroy.

He knows that much of the food we eat each day relies on pollination, but we have a baby in the house, so sorry, bee — you now have a predator.

I hear snap, slap, slip, shit, as co-senior slides around the kitchen in his slip and slide socks. We don't wear shoes in the house as — don't you know — germs are not good for a new baby.

I'm thinking co-senior is practicing his new ballroom dancing steps, but 'thwack' and 'got it' and silence, and I realize that terminator has been successful, and we can all now sleep again at night.

I think back to my mum.

We used to raise our eyebrows after three days and wave goodbye vigorously when she boarded her jet plane.

It wasn't that we didn't love her, but the three-day rule still stands.

And now we are here in our own family's home, and my God, we have been here for six weeks, and if the three-day rule still stands for us, then we are most certainly now fermented herring.

ICONS

Co-senior arrived home this morning with a spring in his step.

I thought this was a bit unusual, as he had been battling the traffic to book his car in for service before the early-morning bedlam commenced.

He told me that he had struck up a conversation with the mechanic. They had bantered about motor vehicles and retirement. The mechanic asked his age, to which he replied, 'What do you think?'

The reply was a definitive 'Forty-seven'.

I emitted a silent guffaw but thought better for fear of self-esteem damage. I quietly muttered under my breath, 'He should have gone to Specsavers!'

Co-senior stood tall as he puffed up his chest, and I couldn't have loved him more. He has run companies, he has run marathons, he has mentored young 'uns, he has given tirelessly and anonymously. He is my first and foremost icon, and by the way, he is way way way past forty-seven.

Next, I was reading about sky jumping.

So, which of you daring Boomers would like to jump out of a plane?

We have lived a good life and don't fear anymore, do we?

Irene O'Shea did, and guess what? She was one hundred and two years old.

Yes, this is not a typo—it *is* one hundred and two.

Sometimes we find it hard to get up from the chair, and she is skydiving!

And she only took up this new sport at the age of one hundred!

Do you still have goals to achieve, Boomers? I am sure you still have megawatts of time to do this.

Not only did this superstar satisfy her thrill-seeking spirit, but she also raised awareness and funds for motor neuron disease in honour of her daughter who died of the disease. She turned tragedy into triumph in her quest to help others. All this in a blossomed age.

Madam Carmel (not 'carnal') ran a chicken farm and boat-hire business but found as a widow she needed to make a better living and chose to be a little unconventional. Hence, the opening of the Pink House, or Questa Casa, in Kalgoorlie, Australia.

Her modus operandi was steeped in etiquette while ensconced in the naughty bordello. Mama Bear supremo she was, for her home of hustlers.

No, you didn't guess right, Boomers—Madam Supreme was eighty.

Imagine finding fame at eighty-three. Well, Iris Apfel did. This eccentric irreverent stormed through the fashion industry carrying her wrinkles (so she said) as a band of courage.

She was born in 1921, wears oversized sunglasses with aplomb, is fearless in her uniqueness, loudly announcing that 'when the fun goes out of dressing, you might as well be dead'. This all the while being married to her husband, Carl, for sixty-seven years.

Yes, you go, girl!!!

Now, did you know that my namesake Julia drove through Africa? Her partner died, and in the depths of thinking there wasn't much life left, she said, 'I feel like I'm 36 from the shoulders up and 146 from the shoulders down, and I wanted the younger me to win for once.'

And off she went, fully armed with inoculations for any infectious disease that you could pronounce. 'Gogo' (grandmother) was on her way to experience the exhilaration and majesty of Africa.

Truck drivers ushered her to the front of the queue while African cultures embraced the wisdom of age. She decided to travel through Africa to London. She would not be halted by the notion that adventure was only for the young.

Julia Alba was eighty years old.

Co-senior and I recently hit the tennis courts.

I had subtly been bragging about my tennis prowess, having attended countless tennis opens in my youth and 'entitledly' home-coached on a grass tennis court on our home property.

School holidays were filled with tennis camps creating first team material, and I swaggered onto the court in confidence ready to smash our opponents out of the game.

Well, how wrong could I be?

Firstly, has the tennis racquet become a whole lot heavier, or is the wrist a whole lot weaker?

Why is it so damn heavy to hold the head level? It took both hands and miss and miss hit of the oncoming speedy groundstrokes.

Had everyone got better, and I had got so much worse? Then the serve followed, but my shoulder wouldn't acquiesce. It was a clickathon of rusty ligaments and no slams into unreturnable corners. Dislocation was imminent, and don't speak to me about running—my brain was most definitely not connecting with my feet.

Ah, then celebrate Margaret Fisher, a pensioner who had her eye on the World Championship Tennis Singles Gold—for senior citizens, of course.

She also had a little quirk in her serving practice partner by the name of Coach Leo. Coach Leo is her border collie, and Margaret was eighty-nine years old.

And then how about Johanna Quaas, with jaw-dropping gymnast skills? She cross trains, hikes, swims, and dances. She is a great grandmother with callouses on her hands, and she is still astounding crowds.

Johanna was born in 1925!

So, co-senior and I are continually lectured by our family about the benefits of yoga. We get it. It is life changing, along with the 'Om' in meditation and the 'Mind' in mindfulness.

We did join a class once just to have a little sticky beak and to shut the chillies up once and for all.

It was all going quite well until it was time for headstands. We are good at giving it a go, but standing on the head is just a bit tricky.

It's not so much the head on the ground thing, it's trying to shoot the legs up into the air thing to land against the wall above thing. It's just trying to get there and to stay perpendicular before a brain explosion.

Forget about the wide-leg derivative or eagle-leg impossibility. There is a lot of push and grunt and sway, but the legs just don't rise above the expansive derriere. The blithe instructor floats over and does her weekly weightlifting training just in that one leg lifting moment, and we are up.

My neck is not happy, and all I can think about is the cost of the physio tomorrow to straighten up the bones and a sticky note to myself that it's time for Weight Watchers to rebalance the body dimensions and move more to the top half.

So, Tao Porchon-Lynch—all hero to you.

Part of your plan is to '*wake up before the sun, be grateful and optimistic, don't put off until tomorrow what you can do today, remember the true meaning of yoga, if you see a barrier try to push past it, do what you love and do not be afraid of aging.*'

You are a yoga master, Tao, and you are a legend. You were born in 1918.

And now, I am writing this book.

So did Alice Munro, revered worldwide as the master of the short story. She feared she didn't have the talent to be a writer, suffering from writer's block and anxiety. Nothing halted her, and she won the Nobel Prize in Literature at the age of eighty-two.

And what about Robert Redford (b:1936), Morgan Freeman (b:1937), Jack Nicholson (b:1937), Donald Sutherland (b:1935), Michael Caine (b:1933), William Shatner (b:1931), Olivia De Havilland (b:1916), Sydney Poitier (b:1927), David Attenborough (b:1926), Tippi Hedren (b:1930), Clint Eastwood (b:1930), Sean Connery (b:1930)—all still living while I am writing this book.

Come on, Boomers, become your own icon.

Plug that chord into the wall of life and living, and plug it in hard. Then remember to switch it on.

I am writing this for you, as we are still in our infancy of pursuing our desires. I read the above and...

I am inspired and inspirational.

I am nervous and I am nerveless.

I am cowardly and I am courageous.

I am frightened and I am free.

I am a Boomer and I am bold.

It's your turn now. Show me what you can do.

SACRIFICE AND RESENTMENT

CO-SENIOR AND I LIVED THE GOOD LIFE IN SOUTH AFRICA.

We lived in a beautiful home.

We had help in the home.

Our family was close and connected and all around.

We could jump on a plane at a whim to fly to Sun City (a luxury resort outside of Johannesburg) to attend concerts.

We revelled in live performances of Leo Sayer, Barry Manilow, Anne Murray, and the list goes on.

We were financially secure, socially connected, and life was good.

However, we were also at the end of home invasions, violent riots, machetes, and really nasty stuff, and we knew it was time.

Co-senior had taken me on a trip 'Down Under' for our honeymoon.

I have to admit I was thinking red wine in Italy or camel rides in the Middle East, but he was certain that the 'Land of Oz' would match up to all expectations.

He had a purpose, and this was the start of manoeuvering my brain into realizing that we could have a safer future where freedom and mateship were tangible.

My feelings were initially of horror as I tried to work out how I would survive the daily routine of housekeeping and social isolation from all that I had.

I had worked hard at keeping connected with those whom I loved, as the natural attrition from marriage breakdown had sorted out the faithful from the divided, and there were many casualties along the way.

I was a creative, a musician, a school captain — I had it all but had nothing if I didn't realize that my family now was my team, and as a team, we all stick together.

On arrival in a new country, with nothing but our suitcases, our children, and potential, we started all over again.

Those were happy times.

It made me realize that four knives and forks sufficed and sleeping on mattresses on the floor was actually like school camp and was warm and connected.

I had no understanding of the laundry process, and we all wore olive green for the first six weeks as all our clothing had also combined as a team in the washing machine, no discrimination, and blended into one ugly 'you don't know what you are doing or wearing' camouflage green.

Poor co-senior went out to show his wares to the business community in debilitating heat with only the front panel of his shirt ironed.

Jacket was an essential to hide the fact that this wasn't my strong point, but he never complained. A divorce nearly ensued when clean washing was mixed with the dirty, but we muddled through, layering down from fancy cordon bleu meals to good old chops and salad.

School parents were kind to us as we enrolled at new schools.

Partner's friends from a previous life were not so kind to us as they completely ignored and were threatened that there was a new chick around.

We moved between cities to conserve our capital, and renting and moving was our way of life as we saved for our own home.

Co-senior sprung a leak north of the border as it was so hot, and I strutted my wild and wooly curls that couldn't be tamed in the sticky humidity.

The children who were ready and packed to move every couple of years wondered why the cycle didn't continue when we took a deep breath and eventually bought and landed safely.

We worked hard, we played hard, we 'familied' hard, we loved hard, and we sacrificed hard.

In those mid years, it all is hard.

It is like an orientation course of providing and intermeshing the family's lives and interests into one big ball. The ball spins in anticipation of each new season and expands and accelerates to accommodate what life throws at it.

It starts spinning out of control in the melee of rugby and netball and debating and swimming carnivals and parent-teacher meetings and the whole 'enchilada' of being a family. And included is the add-on of incessant technological interruption.

Life spins in these middle years for everyone, as they shake in their anxiety and dizziness and reach for solace of valium or red wine, all in the pretence that we all are coping just fine.

We survived and are at the other end now, and we reflect.

We had children whom we cared for and loved deeply.

We bought their shoes before ours.

We paid for their extra-mural activities before our own courses.

We halted our own creativity so they could explore theirs.

We had strong generational debates about issues that now are in the mainstream of life.

And then—*Poof!*—they are gone.

They fly the coop to explore and experiment and find what we found and start the whole cycle again.

We look at each other and ask, 'What was that all about? Where are they now?'

Why didn't we factor in us as well when we were hurled into this vortex of life?

Where was our balance?

Now, without our mini mes, times can be lonely and still and sad.

But life spins around again in the joy of weddings and babies and phone calls and catch ups and the new 'Circle of Life' that mimics our own, and we don't feel so bad as we pick up our guitars and saunter off to lessons with the hunk at the local music school.

Maybe the timing wasn't right then, but sure as hell it is now.

Come on co-senior, I am off to belt out 'Hotel California' in the senior's band at the local music academy. Come with me — you just need to find your newly acquired 'bucket list' shiny black bass guitar.

WHEN WE
WERE YOUNG

━━━━

I REMEMBER THE SMELL OF AFRICA.

It never leaves.

I have lived in Australia for over thirty years, and it's not that I crave to return, it's just in my birth blood—deep, primal, alluring, simple, familial.

My birth arrival was not going to surreptitiously interrupt the colonial lifestyle of my parents.

We were entrenched in 'Gone with the Wind' lifestyle with sweeping stairways and white uniformed employees with shiny red sashes serving dinner on elegant Wedgewood or Royal Doulton and Crystal and Christofle.

We were private schooled in hoity-toity dormitories and bowed in obedience to avoid the cane from disciplinarian parents.

This was all we knew and, in our innocence, believed that all lived this way, as we skipped through our cloistered, privileged existence.

Life was joyful as we played hopscotch and jacks and cars and rode our bikes to the supermarket 'trees' to talk to our imaginary friends.

We ran barefoot down uneven sandy paths to little backstreet cafes to spend minimal amounts on Pez candies and their unique dispensers.

We skipped back after visiting the Greensleeves van and dripped ice cream down our fronts and 'high fived' the greengrocer delivering the weekly order.

I remember sneaking out of the back gate of our house to run up to the neighbouring prestigious Club's polo fields.

There I would nuzzle my favourite polo ponies, who almost swallowed my hand in their attempt to eat my apple, and meet and greet with the Argentinian polo players who galloped in between 'chuckers' to swop steeds.

And then, it was home to bed to be woken early to the sound of the bugle and the bark of the pack of hounds as they waited in anticipation to be let loose to chase a poor fox.

I would spend some evenings around the campfire, shoeless, cutlery-less, while dunking mealie pap (maize meal) into tomato stew, cuddled warmly by my second mumma while teaching me how to click in Xhosa.

Holidays were an adventure.

It would take days to arrive at our destination as we opened and shut gates along the highway to get to the next town.

A Hessian bag hung and swung from the front of the car filled with water in case of disaster.

Peanut butter and Bovril sandwiches and Turkish delight and Coconut Ice tempted our boredom, and the guitar waited in expectation to join the serenade to keep the family from shut eye.

Destinations included swimming and sun and laughter and food and games and walks and freedom.

Game reserves with early morning starts and dump toilets taught us that spiders and snakes sometimes choose smelly homes.

We watched baboons stealing lion cubs, powerless to help, and rhinos locking horns in their fight for supremacy.

We saw lions in waiting of unsuspecting buck and were charged in full force by a mother elephant protecting its calf who had crossed the road before us.

Our windows stayed open, and our doors always welcomed. Chimes greeted the wind embracing our good fortune.

It was so very fortunate and childhood heaven.

And then we noticed the spirit of change seeping into our young adulthood, and it wasn't looking so good.

It was no longer safe to saunter down to the local café, as we noticed we were followed on one of our jaunts. On buying our lollies, we were surrounded by gangs that had broken and entered and were fearful that we had seen them and were a thwart to their plan.

It took quick thinking and diversion to get home safely, but the rumbles had started, and we were feeling the change.

The sounds of the hounds were no longer present, just the scream of a gang rape on the same terrain that curdled our consciousness, never to be forgotten.

Our home was invaded, with furniture removed and television leads hanging desolately as they hung in their incompleteness.

The clothes I cherished were never more to be seen. My charm bracelet with each emotional memory attached in each link was now just the memory left in my brain. My recipes were removed.

I ask myself why?

(Maybe my apple pie hand-me-down was too irresistible to leave.)

The feeling of violation was nasty, but our lives were still intact, even though I received a call with a voice telling me what I was wearing and wouldn't live out the day.

Our car broke down in a dangerous area where a family had been necklaced (tyre around the neck and set alight) and wiped out in burning rubber flames.

A thief stood on my bed in the middle of the night with his light badly disguised, ready to take what he could or bash out my brains.

A woman was dissected at the entrance to home, and traffic lights were not safe if you stayed still too long.

Oh, yes, our indulgence and glorious unawareness had now flipped the coin, but Australia welcomed us and loved us and gave us back our tangible freedom.

We will always be grateful, and we know we are lucky.

We understand our privilege, and in our senior years will give it all back.

MY THERAPIST SAYS...

LET ME START BY SAYING........ THERAPY SAVES LIVES!!

This is a big subject and I don't claim to know anything about it, other than observation. However, in the light of being absolutely authentic here and also generalizing, which is absolutely not politically correct, we older generation are inclined to think that therapy is self-indulgent bitch talk to an impartial professional secret keeper.

There, said it!

(OK, so I am waiting for the floodgates of retort and abuse to begin, but wait a sec and read on—I am now the converted.)

To elaborate, we were brought up with the social stigma that problems and mental health issues hide away very deep down in never-to-be-opened 'hidey holes', never to be found again.

We would never talk openly about struggles. We always kept our saneness or insanity well out of the public domain.

Of course, we faced all the issues that are faced today, and we were lucky then as we didn't have to contend with the power force technological eruptions that now incessantly overcharge the brains of this current generation and everyone else.

Now there is a 'generation therapy'.

Things are changing fast, and millennials are at the forefront of pioneering the value in taking care of their mental health issues and their minds.

This generation is not afraid in their openness.

They display it all on social media and with this element of openness have no fear in discussing their issues about anxiety and feelings. It is normal and natural to visit a therapist to ensure that they learn why they are suffering and how to strategize out of it.

We were young once.

We also had problems then.

Our methodology was seeking help from friends and parental figures, but we had to be poked to be a little bit brave.

We felt resilient and stoic and were taught this way from parents who had to 'soldier on' after surviving the ravages of World War II.

Looping on issues and uncivil behaviour was just as prevalent and never altered its spin in meshing into our anxieties and behaviours.

The generation now is better at asking for help and recognizing, along with meditation and yoga and exercise and healthy eating, that therapy is part of the whole and is so essential to go back to balance in understanding their whys.

There are a myriad of professional educated therapists—yes, real professionals who can turn anxious minds around and life save in some situations.

There is no judgement, as one could potentially find from a bowling, bridge, or golfing partner.

Although, I must say, if trust is involved, these communal friends can hastily bring cognizance to the fact that we are sometimes just being silly, and we walk away with a diffused complication.

JULIE SURSOK

Our generation, however, is now learning that situations and the understanding of deeper issues, need to be tackled by trained professionals and not a 'get together' on a Sunday afternoon.

So, let's look at therapy.

From what I understand (and I could be absolutely off the mark), it is not really a therapist's job to give you advice. The real role of therapy is to get to know yourself better and change your way of thinking or behaving—a facilitator of sorts that navigates one around one's issues and brain. They are there to help one understand the part of the brain that encodes threatening events into memories and the part of the brain that stores emotional memories displaying distinct fears of specific things or experiences.

So, does this perpetual inward-looking discussion perpetuate the problem or solve it?

I don't know, but common sense would say that with tools and regularity, understanding, and therapist fit, therapy is essential.

Talking to some in my research, some swear by therapy.

It is different strokes for different folks.

For some, it has saved their sanity and their lives, as they relinquish their trust to these professional secret keepers. For others, they search hard for the right fit so as not to give away their power but learn to have the power on their own.

We are from a different generation, more protective of our inadequacies or reserved in being authentic for fear of this judgement or gossip.

Our anxieties are different, spanning isolation and monetary issues and health and death and after fifty 'I am free and divorced but now what' issues.

We learn from our experiences and share with our true and trusted friends to find a broader perspective on how we behave because of past and deep scars.

We don't like the notion that we may be Googled or Facebooked for a deeper understanding of us, and we wonder if the therapist sees their own therapist when they need to offload some of the sad and desperate stories that enter their rooms every day.

Don't get me wrong, I do think that therapy is a lifesaver when it is completely and utterly the right fit.

I would hope that a parental body or family member would always have the first interests of their offspring or family at heart and would be wonderful listeners and nurturers for those who are hurting if they only took the chance.

However, families are not usually mental health experts and simply come from a premise of love and care.

So, my conclusion is:

Therapists are professionals.

Therapists are lifesavers.

Therapists can help recognize patterns in your life.

Therapists can help devise better reactions.

Therapists are trust.

Therapists are vital.

It's natural to really like your therapist, to form a close relationship, and to want to become a friend. But the therapist gets paid, and this is not paid friendship.

Therapy is a positive, accepted, necessary, professional role that our generation believes should never inadvertently cross the line in friendship by making Facebook comments on Saturday night attire nor endeavour to usurp the utmost familial roles in the forming of their circle of trust.

Therapy for some is a culture, therapy for others is crucial, and then for some, a religion, and my therapist says…

SOCIAL MEDIA IS NOW MY COMPANION

YES, I GOT IT.

We used to be social, and we made companions.

No, I think I got it wrong.

Now we are conjoined; social media is now our companion.

For us Boomers, it's kinda sad. But what you may not know is that we are the fastest social media adopters, and don't be surprised if you see us popping up where you maybe don't want us to go.

Population aging and social media interaction are now a global phenomenon.

How about that!

We should be proud of ourselves. We now go hand in hand.

You, you little networks of content, are 'tizzling' and touching us in our increasing isolation, but you have burst through as our hero and very important ally to keep us relevantly connected. We are learning rigorously and could even become the new Boomer Big Brother. We know how to get in there and voyeur.

Be afraid—be very afraid.

Don't you know that's why you didn't get the last job we advertised?

You drank too much last Saturday night and exposed too much. It was FOLO to your friends, but sorry, FOLO came true.

You lost out on a magnifico position, and it even included a bite of a new Apple!

I know, I know, you non-seniors out there. I know it is so damn frustrating watching us, very slow..w..w..ly pressing what we think we should press.

It is so much easier for you to Grab and Do. But the problem is that you do it so fast.

We can't remember which buttons you pushed, so can't reverse anything that you may think we need, but we just do not.

In fact, it is all entered in the one-handed, one-fingertip tap concerto—so how the hell can we remember?

And when we ask—whew, we could have asked if you shat pink or taxidermied the dog.

When my flip top was laid to rest in cyber pasture, I mourned deeply.

I thought I had entered techno ecstasy and had Captained my communication, but now had to move up to Rear Admiral without any training.

This was now daunting!

And then, looking back at me was the combined contribution family birthday gift, shiny and new, with even a rose gold cover.

Now that was the deal breaker.

Switching on was new beginnings.

There is a manual, of course, but the manual is online, of course, so now we have to learn how to use this additional techno-genius instrument before we learn how to use *this* techno genius instrument.

With all these gizmos around, life is spinning.

We take a quick glance behind us and are almost knocked over by the monumental superhighway chasing us and gaining momentum at such speed that our creaky senior appendages are smashed and engulfed.

It's mind bedlam trying to keep up.

Those closer in age to the digital era can run faster and spin around in the vortex of high-tech heaven. They manage to land firmly amongst new apps, terminology, and systems without a scratch and wait expectantly for the new flood of innovation.

Oh, Boomers, we just have to submit. For us, maybe we don't need all this stuff.

If we ever do need to communicate in hieroglyphics, we can dial a teenage expert. They will sort out in a millisecond.

They are happy, and we are happy as we sit in cosy coffee shops sharing moments and memories with fellow seniors.

We are ordering coffees from an actual body and face, chatting about the world, and have contentedly ensconced ourselves in our seats unawaredly expanding our bandwidths and backends.

AUTHENTICITY
IS DA THANG

—————

AREN'T YOU TIRED OF BULLSHIT?!

The 'my husband bought me a twenty-five-carat diamond ring—stick in your face—we are doing so well bullshit'?

I mean, who really cares. Well, maybe a teeny tiny bit, but that was a long, long time ago.

The experience of agedom knows how to sift through the outer and the inner.

We are smart little bunnies. We know we have a number of days to make the choices that work for us, and we ain't going to waste them on the perverted notion that the look of perfection creates happiness.

It's actually fun punching a hole through this fascia of deceit and find if there is something deeper, profound, interesting, and goddamn real.

Of course, Facebook and Instagram feed the illusion, but if I was to think of the ones who I would like to laugh, eat, drink, and cry with, it's not those manufactured Facebook pretties.

Who would have thought I would still be in contact with all my school friends? This, to note, is half a century on and living in different countries.

It's a half-half situation — half have flown off to other lands, and half have stayed behind.

One fastidious class member has kept us all well-oiled with recounts of each adventure, movement, slip, and spill. And the individual reunions are so very interesting.

Sometimes when living in another country, you feel like you are an immigrant in the new, and when visiting the old, you become an immigrant there as well. It's a confusing situation.

Much more so when the 'movers' have experienced and lived and immersed themselves in other cultures and customs, and the 'remainers' dig in hard to justify their choice of staying right where they are.

Each to their own, I say, but this is where the title subject matter comes in to play.

As kids, we were authentic; we didn't know any better.

Worldly corruption was still at bay — well, at least in our prehistoric era.

We cheered each other on, provided a shoulder for tearful insecurities, and undressed in boarding school dormitories with our dignity laid bare.

We ran around in gym bloomers, talked over peanut butter and brown bread sandwiches, spoke about worms and periods and boys, and were just downright there — present, unadulterated, nothing to hide, authentic.

As you can see, I went to boarding school.

But then, generationally, things begin to change.

Competition becomes 'adultly' keen, and layers of protection grow thick. Cars, status, money, network cover the heart, and politicking in business and life takes over.

We lose authenticity in the haze of growth, and to survive, one needs to be in the game.

How lucky are those who could peel back this shroud and get to the core!

I have recently face-to-faced some of these school connections in my hometown.

Some are still stuck in the illusion of success and social climbing. It's so hard to talk and connect and avoid conflict when surface conversation is the go. Actually, it's so damn boring.

Most of us now are not interested in having; we are much more interested in being, and that premise only evolves through kindness, contentment, and minimal simplicity.

Others arrive and arrange a coffee through their partners, sort of like a business meeting with three available times given—to be confirmed by a 'ping'. A 'ping' used to be associated with Ping-Pong in our day.

Then there are the beauties. There are some who were great pals in the past life, and some we hardly knew. But, boy oh boy, do they turn out to be little gems.

We wear glasses, our hair is thinner and greyer, our bodies are fatter, our minds slower, our gait stiffer, our hearing dimmer, our hearts warmer, our souls deeper, our laughs louder, our friendship stronger—our vulnerability exposed and our authenticity unquestionable.

We are experienced at cutting through the crap.

We are comfortable and content.

And we skip off into the sunset feeling proud that it's all just real.

SOCIAL SECURITY

So, WHEN IS IT TIME TO ASK FOR HELP?

Our upbringing was puritanical; it was 'we will be right' attitude.

We have worked all our lives, very hard and disproportionate, I might say, supported ourselves and our families all our lives and never thought to look for a handout to help us out as financial booming starts to wane.

Then we ask around, and funny, there are a myriad of benefits, payments, and allowances for the disadvantaged and those who have worked out how it all works out. People who look like us and have had lives like us and have aged like us are quite happy to front up to Centrelink (social security office in Australia) to find out if their decades of tax compliance can now give back in their twilight years.

They are not embarrassed, they are not timid, they are not deceptive. They believe it rightly their right.

So, at what stage does one submit? When the electricity bill arrives and it starts a menopausal sweat, or when medical scripts become more frequent and large sums exit the retirement bank balance?

Eventually, it is time, time to call the said government department. Little warning here — get your stuff ready for a long day. Bring it all and your flask filled with high-energy liquid. Even bring your to-do list. Today may be the day when it actually gets done.

The phone remains on speaker as you go through to first responder. Now is the time to touch up the nails, change the washing, pay the accounts, respond to emails, spring clean, and even write another chapter of this book.

You may even be able to pop out to do a quick grocery shop.

But, a little word of warning, pay attention to that little red battery monitor that glints in the peripheral vision. A slight lapse in attention and forgetful eye could catastrophically disconnect, and the whole process starts all over again.

There are other alternatives.

Take a day trip to the said office. I say 'day trip', as the visit could consume a whole day. And make sure to cancel the hair appointment and budget for the parking fine for an unexpected long-stay parking.

Once in there with all number of tickets and numbers in hand, plonk yourself in the third row with your magazine and book and try not to feel a fraud as you glance surreptitiously at the welfare situations right in front of you.

It's a good idea not to compare cases, as some will surely judge you as you pop your LV sixtieth birthday present into the Woollies plastic bag under your chair.

Then you wait… wait… wait… wait.

Some lonely cases are enjoying their only communication this month and so are spreading out the experience.

The consultant is held captive as they describe the meal they are going to cook tonight. Same consultant breaks for tea (workplace rule — no longer than a certain number of hours) and makes note of the next meal break. I am now hungry and don't even have an apple in my bag.

At last our number flashes up on the screen, and we shuffle up to the counter, endorsing the fact that we are our age. And then there are codes and facts and documents and red tape and passwords and forms and income and…

We leave the department more befuddled than before, with instructions to continue the process online.

We forget about the 'too hard' process and file in the pending tray. Weeks turn into months and in our paper spring clean, we find the document winking at us between the senior aquarobic gym receipt and the accountant's tax return bill.

We are ready and assembled to begin the process again, with all the details from our office visit laid out neatly in front of us.

But alas, unbeknown to us, the link has expired, and the passwords are juxtaposed in each other's names, preventing us from entering into this new world. So resignedly we pull out our diaries and pencil in a date to start this process all over again.

There are rewards for reaching senior status, and for this we are eternally grateful.

Opal (contactless fare collecting system in Sydney) and Seniors Card are now working their muscles.

I promise, some computer savvy backpacker will jump up to help when it's time for recharge, even if communication is via hand-and-eye movement.

Movies are more frequent. The flask is always handy for a tot, and I won't tell if you don't.

We deserve these perks. We have worked hard for them, but if it all goes to pot, just take the lotto. It could be your best chance. You may never know, it may be your lucky day, and you will no longer have to pay a mortgage for a script.

You will be financially free and self-sufficient and will never have to walk into welfare ever again.

FAMILY MATTERS

—

MY GRANDMOTHER HAD ALZHEIMER'S. WE USED TO VISIT her in an aged-care facility and take the same set of photos every time. She was joyfully intrigued, and we packed them away and brought them back again the following weekend.

My mother met my father just prior to the Second World War. She fell on the ice at the local ice rink, and he, the eligible, young, handsome doctor on duty, picked her up, and the rest was tickets. They were married for fifty years, called each other 'Duck', wrote poetry, and recalled adventures to their three adolescent children.

With war imminent, my father proposed to my mother, and within a week, they were married and he was gone.

Years later, my mother, with twenty-four-hour's notice, travelled to Cape Town from Johannesburg, boarded a Troop Ship with a two-year-old dragging behind, and traversed the ocean peppered with mines to fall into the arms of my father on reaching Southampton.

The two-year-old traveller slept in an orange box, and everyone's vocal chords were severely inflamed and swollen on docking after trying to herd the onboard bambinos into one spot for fear of seeing them disappear overboard. Soldiers scanned the deck for their loves. Years spent cavorting together was only in their dreams and now was reality. They began again where they had left off.

My mother would recount this story every time we sat down for high tea — colonial South Africa, of course - high tea was fashionable!!!

I so wish I had listened harder with no simultaneous day-dreams, or meditation as they call it today.

Because pfft… it's gone, and only memories remain, and they fade so slowly to oblivion, and all that is left is a piece of material from one of her dresses, the vision of which remains.

We used to call it her 'smiley' dress.

My dad was an artistic, creative, intelligent teacher and mentor who slowly sunk into rigidity imprisoned in his paralysis and the ins and outs of his tremors.

I peeked through the crack in the door as he lay on his bed. His mind lay still but his face anguished as he held his hands tightly together to stop the incessant shaking. Parkinson's is apparently a genetic disease, and each day I look down to see if my dopamine is depleting and genetics are my future.

I said goodbye to him for the last time with a wave from the back window of a motor vehicle on the way to Australia.

I studied his face and drunk in his expression and got lost in his eyes.

'Bye, Daddy darling. We will meet again.'

My brother, a magnificent cardiothoracic surgeon, is eleven years older than me and makes me feel like I am the only jewel in the crown.

He bought me a life-size doll on his first overseas trip repre-senting his country. The doll was so big that the team had to take turns to carry it through airports — sort of made it more special as they handed over this team mascot to a little girl on their return.

16

Eleven years is a big gap in really knowing your sibling, boarding school separating family from an infant sister. There were always different stages to our communication, and it's difficult to achieve catch up to bridge the years. His face is weathering behind cataracts and old age.

Do I know him?

Have I heard him?

Do I know his dreams and his fears?

Have I understood his loves?

My sister (protective older sister) was always there helicoptering at boarding school to make sure that her little sister survived each day. Our parents seaplaned 'round the world while she kept an eye on her little sibling. She was the first provider of Mary Quant and flatmate when I begged to stay over.

She was my parent's favourite and first love, whose gifts were more special than mine and who shared their inner thoughts when I was still in the throes of adolescence.

Seasons change, oceans divide, interests collide, communication fractures and co-joins again after long periods of separation.

This always requires gentle understanding for assimilation into our disparate lives in order to find some line of synergy and similarity.

Be still and listen—it is not one but both of us that are so good. I get that sometimes families are fractious and fractured. Sometimes an olive branch and Mother Teresa loveliness won't cut it.

Sometimes when the pieces are put back together, there is still a crack that needs to be ignored to ensure the relationship doesn't implode once again.

You learn as seniors to avoid emotional reactions that sometimes family members feel they are free to initiate. Emotional protection is important in dialogue.

However, if there is no middle path, a Buddhism saying is 'Once you feel you are avoided by someone, never disturb them again.'

Sometimes blood family is substituted by those who are drawn into your lives through love and connection. These chosen family members co-nourish the spirit and feed the soul of separation and become the family you need and want.

In our aging season, it is time to love.

Family is important, and the light of forgiveness is illuminating, even if it only remains in the heart.

So stop just for a while, young Boomers.

Don't feel angry, cheated, lonely, and deprived if your past doesn't stand up to scrutiny. All parents and family usually just try to do their best.

Share your stories with younger family or adopted family members.

They will love you for it when they begin to stack on the miles.

They will remember your stories and will recount mignons from past family history to their own offspring.

Teach them to listen more.

Teach them to listen harder.

Teach them to share more.

Teach them to question more.

Teach them to philosophize more.

Don't let them lose their heritage and their past.

Don't let them ever regret.

I get it.

Families are complicated.

But

At the end of the day

Family matters.

THE SOURCE

The olive trees in the garden of Gethsemane are the oldest known olive trees. This has been proven by a study conducted by the Italian National Research Council in conjunction with Italian Universities. However, there are five trees in the garden that could not be analyzed. These trees are so gnarled that their trunks are hollowed out—iconic reflections of the torture of pain. Co-senior and I sat amongst these trees, and Jesus was there sitting right beside us. It was plain, it was simple, it was real, and it was clear.

We are now older, becoming more reflective, say, 'what the hell'.

But, subconsciously, let's face it, hidden in there somewhere is maybe that hidden gorge leading us to the search of the clarity of life.

Are we connected to our Spiritual Source?

Are we so engaged in the mental and the physical that we completely bury the spiritual?

Are our minds closed or open?

How are some so sure and some so lost?

Why does the true theologian minister deeply impart their religious message without sitting where we sat, and the vagrant searcher spend their life savings to explore what history has notated?

Eastern spirituality seems to have been preserved throughout the centuries, but over on the other side? Do we question enough? Is 'the source' just a collective unconscious, a higher being? Is it Allah, Brahma, Vishnu, Shiva, Buddha, Jesus, or God? Who knows? Well, for me—I have a strong belief that I know, and I'll let you in to why a little later.

One can throw *atheist* and *agnostic* into the mix, but as I slide slowly into the awe-inspiring journey of discovery, the longing for spiritual meaning provides a calming sense of comfort.

Questions get thrown around about the reason and purpose of life. Some feel we are really just all connected. Funny aside, my daughter rang today after a DNA test. She was elated as she had discovered that we have thousands of DNA-connected relatives all over the world—so maybe there is some premise in that idea.

Getting back to the serious, the question is how do we make peace with our mortality? All kinds of crazies now start to creep in.

As a Christian, would I be forced to await judgement before I knew whether I was going up or down?

So why is good up and bad down?

I mean, 'up' could be hanging out of a plane at thirty thousand feet with one hand, and down could be a luxurious spa off a magical Greek island.

And to wait for judgement—it's like not knowing your seat number on a plane or whether you have an upgrade or whether you are going to be bumped. That would be a complete nightmare for me. I mean, I have to know my seat on the plane, how far away from the toilet, next to the window, right in the middle. So being on guarantee status (the term they use on ships), despite sounding pretty good to me in this instance, is a tad grey.

If the Source leans more to the atheist or agnostic side, then oblivion is the destination. But maybe then again, it's not torturous hell, it's just nothing—*phwoa*— and I'll not even know I'm dead. I'll just exist through the earth, become part of the earth from where I became and become human again.

Oh God, please don't use the fertilizer!!!

One's own beliefs are sometimes born out of experience and moments. For co-senior, it was an unexpected, sacred, warm, engulfing light of love, at the age of eight actually—who has this blessed experience at the age of eight? For me, it was a passage in a city church 'You will be blessed with the breast and the womb' one day before receiving expectant dubious results and finding that I was just that. And the answer to every ponderous question always being found in a passage or a word.

For us personally, our Source is called God.

We need to find God, and he cannot be found in noise and restlessness.

God is the friend of silence. See how nature—trees, flowers, grass—grows in silence? See the stars, the moon, and the sun, how they move in silence…

'We need silence to be able to touch souls', so aptly described by Mother Teresa.

I sat in that garden and looked out over the horizon as the sun's golden rays lit up the vista before me.

The ray beamed over the Church of the Holy Sepulchre, the Wailing Wall, the Dome of the Rock, and my heart, and I knew, positively, affirmatively, loudly, that there was nothing to fear.

We would all grow our own set of wings, whatever shape, size, or religion, and we would all be one on the other side.

YOU'RE NOT A SENIOR TILL YOU THINK YOU'RE A SENIOR

I READ A REPORT THIS MORNING THAT SAID THOSE OF US who think young stay young.

It said:

'The young at heart often insist you are only as old as you feel.

Now a study has proved they are right, finding that those who feel younger than they are show fewer signs of brain ageing.... those who said they felt younger had more grey matter in their brains.' (Daily Telegraph)

So, listen up, seniors, start thinking young. It sounds good to me!

Let's do a little ageless 'think young' work session right now.

Are you thinking twenty-five instead of sixty-five?

Are you wearing red lipstick? Boys, you can wear it too if it floats your boat.

Do you wear red and orange and pink instead of grey and beige?

Are you dancing instead of shuffling?

Is the beat of the music thinking tango sexy?

Can you take it up a notch and think hip-hop—just, maybe?

Can you sing?

Can you sing Adele and Taylor Swift?

Do you know who Adele and Taylor Swift are?

Or maybe can you belt out a Susan Boyle and shock everyone?

Can you sing in public—loud and free? You are not wrapped up in antique binding!

Can you learn an instrument and play it loudly?

Can you laugh—silly, real, interactive laugh?

Have you got a group, not just your age but all ages?

Do you pillow fight on the bed with your grown-up family?

Do you drown in chocolate now and then without any guilt?

Do you sleep dreaming of faraway lands still to visit, even if only in your dreams?

Do you drink good coffee and good wine?

Do you learn today's ways and communicate across generations?

Just imagine for a moment that you did not know what your age was on paper. Imagine you had no passport or birth certificate and your age was simply based on how you felt.

What would be your age?

Are you in the prime of life based on how you feel?

Scientists are finding that some people seem to flourish as they age, while others fade.

'The extent to which older adults feel much younger than they are may determine important daily or life decisions for what they do next,' says Brian Nosek at the University of Virginia.

The older person has a mind that is still oh so fertile. And how lucky are we that we have the experience of age to back up the decisions that we make right now?

Our subjective age will also influence our health so much more than what our identity documents presume.

So come on, seniors, work out what age you feel, reduce it by several years, and you will see there will be lots of benefits here.

My very closest friend is eighty, but she is not eighty.

Does eighty sound advanced to you or just a number, as it should be?

She drives across town in the maniacal congestion that we experience in a big city. She visits her sister on the other side of town and returns well after dark.

When did you last drive through the city on a Friday night in the dark, dear seniors?

She cooks for an army — did I say she was Greek?

She even brings croissants and feta around at four in the morning to watch her nation in the World Cup Soccer, and we all shout 'Opa' together.

I don't think she ever sleeps.

She reads Homer's *Odyssey* and Thucydides and philosophizes about the Pyrrhic Wars. Then she teaches us all about her history, reminding us that everything in the English language is a derivative of hers.

Does she think young? You betcha!!!

We dream together of sitting overlooking the Ionian Sea and visiting the Dodecanese Islands, the Cyclades, the Cretan Islands, the Northern Sporades.

And we will drink Ouzo one day on that piece of land we have talked about and say 'i zoi einai omorfi' (life is beautiful) and gaze into eternity and know we will be there together.

So we have made a pact today, have we, seniors.

We have lots more loving to do

We have lots more exploring to do.

We have lots more sharing to do.

We have lots more giving to do.

We have lots more laughing to do.

We have lots more relating to do.

And we have lots more life to do. Come on, we are all still forty, aren't we?

THE BUCKET LIST

Why is it called the 'bucket list'? 'Bucket list' feels like it's the list-before-you-die list. Everything tips out of the bucket, and boom! you are gone list.

I like the idea of an 'Itch List' much better—those niggly little itches that have cavorted with the soul for possibly centuries and can now be joyfully pursued.

So, what to put on the 'itch list'?

Sometimes the clarity is luminous and sometimes hiding in murky waters.

A good coffee, an empty journal, a silent environment, and the list of dreams become clear.

I don't really get the hellbent, adrenaline-filled crazies list. Are these on the list because it's 'what the hell if you vaporize in the process—who cares, as the days are limited' list? You know, jumping out of planes or swimming in piranha waters or handling king cobras.

Is this really the dream or the 'you see, I'm not doddery accomplishment' to be thrust in the grandbabies faces?

It all feels a bit 'ouch'.

I guess it starts with a dream. What gave the buzz when we were nippers and still does now? What places do we want to see, only touched in coffee table books? What inspires, and does it have to be realistic? Maybe but maybe not.

Is it trite to say you can do anything you want if you want it hard enough?

What do we want?

What do we want to feel?

What do we want to do?

What do we want to give?

So many questions for the soul.

Let's start.

How about…

Route 66 across the US—even better in a convertible. Paul McCartney told us about this journey, even being mistaken for Paul Simon on the way.

Tulips in Amsterdam

Music festivals in Salzburg

Red wine in Puglia

Northern lights in high latitudes

Journey to the inner self in India

Blossoms in Japan

Wildlife in Africa

Wadi to Petra

And then…

Hip-hop classes

Jimmy Choo very high boots (if you can still walk in them)

Flying lessons

Beach horseback riding

Ice skating

Hot air ballooning

Sangria

Save a life

Arrange a family reunion

And more…

Dress in a caftan (with co-senior if there is one)

Shisha smoke in your caftan

Get baptized in your caftan

Wear no underwear in your caftan

Dance unawaredly in your caftan

Take your caftan off and skinny dip—preferably in the Greek Isles as the sun sets.

So much to dream about, reflect on, be inspired by, be philanthropic for.

Start your itch list, my darlings, and itch hard.

Itch till the blood flows, itch till the feeling grows, itch till the glow shows.

Keep on itching—it means you are still alive.

FUTURE

WE ARE THE FUTURE TO THE PAST. NOW ISN'T THAT JUST profound!

Our comparative world is almost like another planet, a planet that we may not recognize ourselves if we could time travel into the future.

As you all know by now, I was a doctor's daughter, very well versed in descriptions of ugly medical conditions while sitting 'round the dinner table.

I saw the end of a power drill rotating towards my mouth.

I saw the black and white parquet hospital flooring and nuns dressed in full garb nursing people back to health.

I trained as a television director and asked my father if I could televise one of his operations. It was allowed so long as we scrubbed up squeaky clean and sterilized. With most of the crew fainting, it wasn't a success, but opened my eyes to the friendly focussed banter that occurs in operating theatres accompanied by the melodious harmonies of Abba or rocking with Elvis.

These days, massive apparitions circle and encase our bodies in investigative procedures with not a human in sight. Diagnostic instruments pin point ailments. Nuclear medicine is brought into play for certain conditions. Eyes can be scanned into the depths of the brain; brains can be healed by brilliant surgical hands.

Advances in pharmaceutical fields have saved millions of lives, and we are all staying alive longer, budgeting out our retirement savings in detail.

But we may be and could be the next group of centenarians if we are offered what is about to come.

We won't have to wait for donors if our organs mutate and give up.

The 3-D printer will just create new ones. These will match our own body parts right down to the very last millimetre.

So, does that mean I can have another glass of wine and more chocolate and a lot more butter on my toast?

Imagine the exciting possibility of scientists being able to create blood vessels, pancreases, and even synthetic ovaries. And may I say with no rejection?

Will robotics replace surgeons? Will surgery be another industry slammed out by advances?

I hope not. I rather like my surgeon holding my hand, whispering controlled encouragement, while my consciousness slowly shuts down for a while.

Today, complex procedures can be performed that may have been highly difficult or impossible before, creating more precision, control, and flexibility.

And how about wireless brain sensors that are placed in the brain and dissolve when they are no longer needed?

And students gaining experience via virtual reality get 'uptight and close' to real life medical experiences. So, the 'Good Doctor' isn't just make believe?

Then the Big G will take hold. It has patented a digital contact lens that will change the course of diabetes management by measuring blood glucose levels from tears.

Go figure.

And forget about Amazon's Alexa and Google Assistant. We will now be offered Google Brain. Well, sometimes my brain does feel googled, but this possible innovation may be able to create our digital self, based on neurological information. We just upload our minds to a computer and live on in digital form.

Oh, please, dear Google Brain, if you are going to play around, I would love an Einstein or a Socrates or even a Nostradamus brain. That would be very cool. I would need a very sharp brain, and you can add in less cellulite, longer legs, and definitely a flat tum.

Pretty please!

And while we ponder on that, when slumberland beckons, a pill bottle will glow blue to advise that it is medication time, and the red bottle glow is not good as, bugger, we have missed a dose.

And there is more for reflection.

Don't we love to travel, and how will supersonic look?

The Golden Age of travel in our parent's past consisted of a ten-day, nine-stopover journey from Africa. It was luxurious and aspirational and well heeled. Drinks were ever flowing, finest dresses, high heels, and pearls were donned, and mile-high adventures with the passenger next door were naughtily initiated.

Well, it was a very long journey, was it not?

The 'Flying Boat' was swathed in cigar and cigarette and pipe smoke, and life was good.

Today, we jet across the world in superjets with industry-leading technology. We are experiencing the Dreamliner effect.

Australia to London is a direct flight wrapped up in our 'trackies' and runners supported by neck pillows and leg pushers and noise cancelling earphones to never ever get to know the passenger next door.

Special discount tickets flood our inboxes, and heaven help us if we have searched a destination. By the time we book we have almost been there with the glut of every known experience or meal flooding our consciousness.

And how about the future—are aircraft going to be longer or wider or faster?

The 777X twinjet by Boeing is in the works. Its length will be enormous and will seat four hundred passengers.

And there is talk about going electric. Cars are moving fast in this direction, and air travel will follow shortly. Flying taxis could become a reality, and pilotless airliners may not seem to be too farfetched.

As an aside, I am glad we invested in lithium.

Could the tailless flying wing show its face again, and will supersonic air travel be developed to fly twenty times faster than the speed of sound and travel at the edge of space?

Hopefully, pressured supersonic earplugs would evolve at the same pace.

And some more observations…

We lost our dog once when we were on vacation and the 'smoke signal' was out. We dialled up an operator from our home with a large speaker-like device against our ear. The operator through-connected to all homes in the area to put out a suburban alert, and our love was found.

Today, these communication items are happily stored in cabinets as antiques.

Mobile phones will be firmly embedded in our daily lives.

Holographic functions will be developed, phones will be folded via flexible frames into two. Our trusty information providers will morph into wristbands, and GPS belt clips and video flat screens, and others.

Heaven forbid, my grandchildren, your parents are addicted already—this is certainly now going to be your best and only friend.

Will we become a brave new world?

Will climate change redistribute our living spaces?

Will cash be as ancient as a reel-to-reel tape?

Will gender become androgynous?

Will food be a perfected nutritional pill? (That would be a pity.)

Will drones be the new ambulance?

Will holiday camps be set up on the Moon and Mars?

As Tony Kushner in 'Millennium Approaches' says…

'Don't be afraid. People are so afraid. Don't be afraid to live in the raw wind, naked, alone…. Learn at least this: What you are capable of. Let nothing stand in your way.'

So, let nothing stand in our way, Boomers.

We are standing right here and right now, and the future will be as natural to our offspring as we exactly were to our past.

SO WHAT HAVE
I LEARNED

IT IS ALL A JOURNEY, AND IT IS WHAT WE MAKE OF IT.

I know for some it can be damn hard. It can be magnificent or macabre. It can be malevolent or marvellous. But it is a journey that we have been gifted. Our outers and inners are unique. We are loved for our souls, not our appearance. Our brains are our strongest weapons, and there are choices everywhere to be made to cherish the steps.

So, what have I learned?

It's hard to do what we fear.

It's hard to take the first step.

It's hard to say no.

It's hard to communicate.

It's sort of hard to not engage with those that bring us down.

It's sort of hard to lie to not hurt others.

It's sort of hard to not judge.

It's sort of hard to stay fit.

It's not hard to listen.

It's not hard to care.

It's not hard to smile.

It's not hard to be kind.

It's not hard to laugh.

It's not hard to share.

It's not hard to love.

It's not hard to have freedom of spirit.

We can all begin, reinvent, and bloom well after the clock has passed the hour.

So, get out there, my Boomers—this life is yours, and it's yours to live.

Don't die before you are dead.

ACKNOWLEDGMENTS

Co-senior who has listened to every idea and read every word of this book over and over again. My husband, Daryl has supported me every step of the way and always encourages me to follow through with what I love to do, and I love him for that.

My children, who are my best friends.

My wonderful launch team who only want my success and have laughed with me along the way. To Patricia, Noel and Lorraine, Nicola, Warren, Ivan, Katrina, Mary. Michelle, who patiently read every word and encouraged me to keep writing.

To the seniors who need help out there to find a warm place to sleep at night—thank you for giving me the Why, and we will try to help change your situation as soon as we possibly can.

Thank you, Liz Smith and 100 covers, with a special mention to Cherub. Thank you to Cory and Wallace at Formatted Books.

Thank you to Leonie and her colleagues.

Thank you to Chandler and your team for helping us believe we can do this. Your persistence paid off and I saw the light. I am so very grateful that I discovered my passion.

And to all my fellow seniors, I would love to meet you and speak with you and share experiences and laugh with you.

Let's stay in contact – I would love to hear your stories.

www.imnowcalledasenior.com

GLOSSARY

Hello Boomers

Grim Reaper: a personification of death in the form of a cloaked skeleton wielding a large scythe

Methusalah: Methuselah is said to have died at the age of 969, making him the longest-lived figure in the Bible. The name Methuselah translates as 'man of the dart'.

Spray and Pray

Ebola: an infectious and frequently fatal disease marked by fever and severe internal bleeding, spread through contact with infected body fluids by a filovirus.

E.coli: a bacterium commonly found in the intestines of humans and other animals, some strains of which can cause severe food poisoning.

Failure to Launch

Casa de los padres: fathers house

Downsizing

Visado residentia: permanent residency

GoGet: Car share network in Australia

Greenshare: Cars for hire by the hour or day

3-2-2: 3 bedroom/2 bathrooms/2 carparks

Trains and Boats and Planes

Boerewors: South African sausage

Seated reverse cowgirl: Sex position

Mile-high Club: The mile-high club is slang for the people who have had sexual intercourse on board an aircraft in flight.

Namaste: Used both for greeting and leave-taking.

Shinkansen: a railway system carrying high-speed passenger trains.

Risky Business: Movie starring Tom Cruise

Macklemore: an American rapper

Shantaram: 2003 novel by Gregory David Roberts

Homeless

Opal Card: Opal is the smartcard ticketing system used to pay for travel on public transport in Sydney, the Blue Mountains, Central Coast, the Hunter, and the Illawarra.

PC: politically correct

I'm Off to Learn Karate

Sudoku: Sudoku is a puzzle in which missing numbers are to be filled into a 9 by 9 grid of squares which are subdivided into 3 by 3 boxes.

Skedonk: an old, battered car

Silence to Healing

Stuttafords: Stuttafords is a high-end retailer of branded fashion, apparel, footwear, accessories and cosmetics, within premium shopping malls in South Africa.

Don't Give Up When Others Do It Better

MasterChef: *MasterChef* is a television competitive cooking show franchise

Ghee: clarified butter made from the milk of a buffalo or cow, used in South Asian cooking.

Medical Checks
Cook Islands: The Cook Islands is a nation in the South Pacific

Stuck in the Middle with You
Gen X Y Z: Generation X (or Gen X) is the demographic cohort following the Baby Boomers and preceding the Millennials. Researchers and popular media typically use birth years ranging from the early-to-mid 1960s to the early 1980s.

A Wee Little Problem
Ivan Origone: The fastest skier on the planet

Friends
Amway: Amway (short for 'American Way') is an American multi-level marketing company

Orgasmic Oldies
Something about Mary: a 1998 American comedy film

Cruise Solution
Christian Grey: Christian **Trevelyan** Grey is the male protagonist of the trilogy, *Fifty Shades of Grey*.

It's OK to be Miserable Now and Then
Lake Louise: Lake Louise is a hamlet in Banff National Park in the Canadian Rockies, known for its turquoise, glacier-fed lake

I'm Magnificently Magnificent
LV Bag: Louis Vuitton Bag
Kumon: Kumon is an educational network created by Toru Kumon, which uses his Kumon Method to teach mathematics and reading for young students.

Radio to Netflix
Whitehall to Trafalgar Square: Destinations in the UK displayed on a Monopoly Board

Death
Musgrave and Watson: Travel Agency
Demtel: television infomercials

Be Fearless about your Flaws
MYOB: Mind Your Own Business, is an Australian multinational corporation that provides tax, accounting and other business services software to small and medium businesses.

What Every Grandparent Should Know
Lamingtons: a square of sponge cake dipped in melted chocolate and grated coconut.

The Taste, Sound, and Smell of Memory
PTS: PTS is a common, normal, and often adaptive response to experiencing a traumatic or stressful event.

Family Matters
Mary Quant: iconic fashion designer of the 1960s.

You're Not a Senior Till You Think You're a Senior
Pyrrhic wars: The Pyrrhic War was a war fought by Pyrrhus, the king of Epirus.

Future
The Good Doctor: American drama series
Amazon's Alexa: a virtual assistant developed by Amazon

Google Assistant: Google Assistant is an artificial intelligence-powered virtual assistant developed by Google

Google Brain: Google Brain is a deep learning artificial intelligence research team at Google

Thank You for Reading My Book!

I really appreciate all your feedback and
I love hearing what you have to say.

If you enjoyed reading *I'm Now Called a Senior WTF*,
a review on Amazon is always very well received and appreciated.

Thank you so much!

Julie Sursok

www.imnowcalledasenior.com

Made in the USA
Coppell, TX
25 April 2020